BENN PITMAN
AUTHOR AMERICAN PITMAN SHORTHAND

The New Practical

SHORTHAND

== MANUAL ==

A COMPLETE *and Compre-*
hensive Exposition of
PITMAN SHORTHAND
adapted for use in Schools, Col-
leges and for Home Instruction

REVISED EDITION

Copyright, 1892
CARNELL & HOIT
Albany, N. Y.

PREFACE.

With every great revolution comes the necessity for a change of means and methods adapted to the new condition of affairs. The great revolution in business which has been wrought by the general introduction of shorthand and typewriting in office work, found the mechanism of schools entirely inadequate for the suitable preparation of stenographers. Improvement has been made, but still every good book for instruction in shorthand is a boon both to teachers and to those who propose to make stenography their means of earning a living or winning an honorable record in the great army of high-class workers. If excuse were needed, this is our only excuse for presenting the New Practical Manual of Shorthand. It gives the general principles of the Pitman system, with such changes as time and use have proved most necessary, and outlines a method of teaching shorthand which is the outgrowth of long experience. It is confidently believed that the diligent student will find in the following pages a smooth road to the acquisition of a successful and fascinating study.

NOTE TO REVISED EDITION. — The cordial endorsement which has been given to this book by Shorthand teachers, together with the results of its work in our own school, as shown in the successful careers of our Shorthand students, have led us to undertake a revision of its contents, by which we have improved some important features of the original and added about twenty-five pages of new material.

We now present this revised edition with the hope that it may continue the good work already accomplished by the earlier editions.

CONTENTS.

	PAGE.
Introduction, - - - -	v
Elementary Sounds, -	1
Exercise on Analysis, -	2
Consonant Alphabet, -	7
Joined Consonants, - -	13
First Position Vowels, -	14
Second " " -	17
Third " " -	19
Use of Upward and Downward *r*, - - -	21
Use of Upward and Downward *l*, - - -	22
Review Exercises, - -	22
Circle *s* and *z*, - - -	24
Circle *sez*, - - - -	26
Review Exercises, - -	26
Loops *st*, *zd* and *str*, -	28
When to use Circles and Loops, - - - -	30
The Initial *w* Hook, -	32
Semicircles *w* and *y*, -	32
Heavy *m*, - - - -	34
Tick *h*, - - - - -	34
Review Exercises, - -	36
Word-signs (1st list), -	37
Phrases, - - - -	38
Word-signs (2d list), -	40
Word-signs (3d list), -	42
Straight Double Consonants, - - - -	42
Curved Double Consonants, - - - -	46
Triple Consonants, - -	48
The *n* Hook, - - - -	50
The *f* or *v* Hook, - -	52

	PAGE.
S Added to Final Hooks, - - - -	52
Double Con. Word-signs,	54
Ticks, *the*, *a*, *an* and *and*,	54
Review Exercises, - -	56
The Large *w* Hook,	57
Ml, *nl*, *rl*, and *lr*, - -	58
The Large Final Hooks,	60
The *s-shun* curl, - - -	60
The Halving Principle,	62
The Doubling Principle,	66
Special Vocalization, -	66
Word-signs (5th list), -	68
Half-length Word-signs,	70
Prefixes and Affixes, -	72
Word-signs (7th list), -	74
Review Exercises, - -	76
Table of Appendages, -	78
Table of Word-signs, -	80
Formation of Outlines,	84
Consonant Outlines, -	88
Contracted Outlines, -	92
Phrasing, - - - -	94
Conclusion, - - - -	103
Writing Exercise, - -	104
Material for Practice, -	128
Punctuation, - -	128
Business Letters, - -	129
Legal Testimony, -	140
Eulogy on Washington, - - - -	144
Self-Reliance, - - -	146
Exercises in Shorthand,	148
Abbreviations, - - -	168
Phrases, - - - -	170

INTRODUCTION.

The system presented on the following pages is that of Pitman, with the addition of the Munson hook for *thr* and a few other modifications which have been found of special value. It is not, however, to add to the already large number of systems that this work has been prepared, but to present principles already well established, in such a manner that they may be the most easily learned, and used with the best possible results. To this end, the principles have been arranged in the most natural order, and are illustrated by outlines for words as they are actually used in reporting, so that the student does not learn one form, and then find, in some subsequent lesson, that it is necessary to change for some other form.

As phonography is a representation of the sounds of the language, it is necessary that the student learn to recognize sounds quickly and correctly. The exercises on analysis of words have proved of great value in this respect. The vowels are classified as finally to be used, in this way avoiding a large amount of unnecessary work, and the confusion, in the mind of the student, that has heretofore resulted from the fact that he learned the vowels as *long*, *short*, and *diphthongs*, and when they were well in mind, found it necessary to dispense with that division and learn them in a different order; namely, *first, second,* and *third position.* As it is very desirable that first impressions be correct, and as the first thing necessary to determine in writing shorthand is the position of the accented vowel of each word, it follows that the only division of the vowels which the student should know, is that of position. This new grouping of the vowels prevents much hesitation in writing, as well as much illegibility.

The position of outlines is also taught from the beginning, so that the old stumbling blocks " Corresponding Style " and " Reporting Style " are removed. No change is made from the former to the latter, but the whole scheme is a gradual development of the reporting style. Throughout the book, great emphasis is put upon *legibility,* and the use of the various appendages is so presented as to contribute very materially to this important object, as well as to the other requirement of phonography; namely, *speed.* Unnecessary and difficult word-signs have been eliminated, yet enough are given for the most rapid work.

The principles of phrasing and the formation of outlines are so explained and illustrated as to make it possible for the student to develop the utmost skill in reporting.

ELEMENTARY SOUNDS.

1. An alphabet should have a character for each elementary sound of the language it professes to represent. If any considerable speed is desired in writing, these characters should be the simplest possible, and the most easily formed should be assigned to the most frequently occurring sounds.

2. A moment's thought will readily show that the longhand in common use is very defective in all the above particulars. It is most ridiculous to teach young children that *k-n-o-w* spells *no ; w-e-i-g-h-e-d, wad ; a-c-h-e, ak ; s-t-r-a-i-g-h-t, strat ; p-h-l-e-g-m, flem ;* or even *t-a-k-e, tak.* Attention is called to this unreasonable mode of spelling in order that a perfect alphabet may be better understood and appreciated.

3. The basis upon which the present system of shorthand is constructed is that each elementary sound is always represented by the same character, and that a given character shall always represent the same sound. The spelling, therefore, is entirely phonetic and without any regard to longhand. Thus, the word *w-e-i-g-h-e-d* is written with the marks which represent the sounds of *w-a-d ; a-c-h-e,* with those which represent the sounds of *a* and *k ;* and all other words in the same manner.

4. Before a word can be written in shorthand it must be analyzed — that is, separated into its elementary sounds — and in order that the student may learn to do this readily, the Exercise on Analysis of Words should be thoroughly practiced.

5. The consonants should not be pronounced as in long-hand, but should be given the exact sounds as heard in words ; e. g., do not say *be*, and *de*, but the pure consonant sounds as heard at the end of *ebb* and *aid*. The vowels should also be pronounced precisely as heard in the words in which they are used. Thus, *bad* should not be spelled *be-ă-de*, but, *b-ă-d*.

6. All words given in the exercise below should be studied as follows : 1. Pronounce the word distinctly and correctly. 2. Sound the elements slowly. 3. Cover the "word" column with a slip of paper and pronounce the elements until the correct word is suggested. 4. Cover the "ele-ments" column and analyze the words. Rapid analysis is necessary in writing shorthand. Correct synthesis is essential in reading shorthand. Therefore, the student should not hurry over these words, but, on the other hand, give them his *very best attention*.

Exercise on Analysis of Words.

Word.	*Elements.*	*Word.*	*Elements.*
make	m-ā-k	came	k-ā-m
take	t-ā-k	same	s-ā-m
lake	l-ā-k	jail	j-ā-l
rake	r-ā-k	sail	s-ā-l
bake	b-ā-k	chaise	sh-ā-z
shake	sh-ā-k	bathe	b-ā-th
name	n-ā-m	wait	w-ā-t
fame	f-ā-m	days	d-ā-z
gale	g-ā-l	age	ā-j

Word.	Elements.	Word.	Elements.
lathe	l-ā-th	paw	p-ạ
rage	r-ā-j	talk	t-ạ-k
maze	m-ā-z	chalk	ch-ạ-k
Yale	y-ā-l	bought	b-ạ-t
sake	s-ā-k	caught	k-ạ-t
chain	ch-ā-n	fall	f-ạ-l
mat	m-ă-t	tall	t-ạ-l
rat	r-ă-t	fawn	f-ạ-n
nap	n-ă-p	thaw	th-ạ
catch	k-ă-ch	dawn	d-ạ-n
gag	g-ă-g	gnaw	n-ạ
thatch	th-ă-ch	gall	g-ạ-l
smash	s-m-ă-sh	thorn	th-ạ-r-n
that	th-ă-t	paws	p-ạ-z
vamp	v-ă-m-p	pause	p-ạ-z
hatch	h-ă-ch	gauze	g-ạ-z
bank	b-ă-ng-k	wroth	r-ạ-th
thank	th-ă-ng-k	feet	f-ē-t
tank	t-ă-ng-k	meat	m-ē-t
far	f-ä-r	team	t-ē-m
jar	j-ä-r	beat	b-ē-t
palm	p-ä-m	ream	r-ē-m
calm	k-ä-m	leap	l-ē-p
dark	d-ä-r-k	teaze	t-ē-z
park	p ä-r-k	seize	s-ē-z
farm	f-ä-r-m	weep	w-ē-p
czar	z-ä-r	thee	th-ē
arm	ä-r-m	these	th-ē-z
harm	h-ä-r-m	shear	sh-ē-r
hark	h-ä-r-k	heath	h-ē-th
yard	y-ä-r-d	teeth	t-ē-th
psalm	s-ä-m	year	y-ē-r
saw	s-ạ	ease	ē-z

Word.	Elements.	Word.	Elements.
pet	p-ĕ-t	hit	h-ĭ-t
fetch	f-ĕ-ch	dig	d-ĭ-g
met	m-ĕ-t	fill	f-ĭ-l
desk	d-ĕ-s-k	still	s-t-ĭ-l
yet	y-ĕ-t	list	l-ĭ-s-t
cent	s-ĕ-n-t	ship	sh-ĭ-p
wet	w-ĕ-t	chip	ch-ĭ-p
sent	s-ĕ-n-t	dish	d-ĭ-sh
saith	s-ĕ-th	ditch	d-ĭ-ch
then	th-ĕ-n	witty	w-ĭ-t-ĭ
egg	ĕ-g	thin	th-ĭ-n
death	d-ĕ-th	sing	s-ĭ-ng
tenth	t-ĕ-n-th	this	th-ĭ-s
gem	j-ĕ-m	live	l-ĭ-v
check	ch-ĕ-k	note	n-ō-t
shell	sh-ĕ-l	rote	r-ō-t
yellow	y-ĕ-l-ō	wrote	r-ō-t
vent	v-ĕ-n-t	boat	b-ō-t
pile	p-ī-l	goat	g-ō-t
mile	m-ī-l	joke	j-ō-k
dime	d-ī-m	doze	d-ō-z
fine	f-ī-n	sows	s-ō-z
kind	k-ī-n-d	wore	w-ō-r
tithe	t-ī-th	yore	y-ō-r
smile	s-m-ī-l	fop	f-ŏ-p
chime	ch-ī-m	shop	sh-ŏ-p
vine	v-ī-n	knot	n-ŏ-t
wind (v.)	w-ī-n-d	dog	d-ŏ-g
pyre	p-ī-r	volley	v-ŏ-l-ĭ
wire	w-ī-r	shoddy	sh-ŏ-d-ĭ
vice	v-ī-s	lodge	l-ŏ-j
dip	d-ĭ-p	watch	w-ŏ-ch
pit	p-ĭ-t	yon	y-ŏ-n

Word.	Elements.	Word.	Elements.
yacht	y-ŏ-t	cup	k-ŭ-p
food	f-ōō-d	judge	j-ŭ-j
ooze	ōō-z	thumb	th-ŭ-m
noose	n-ōō-s	bur	b-ŭ-r
cool	k-ōō-l	pug	p-ŭ-g
boom	b-ōō-m	sir	s-ŭ-r
moon	m-ōō-n	young	y-ŭ-ng
boot	b-ōō-t	were	w-ŭ-r
hoot	h-ōō-t	vision	v-ĭ-zh-ŭ-n
poor	p-ōō-r	verse	v-ŭ-r-s
rouge	r-ōō-zh	won	w-ŭ-n
goose	g-ōō-s	one	w-ŭ-n
booth	b-ōō-th	murky	m-ŭ-r-k-ĭ
took	t-ŏŏ-k	buzz	b-ŭ-z
shook	sh-ŏŏ-k	does	d-ŭ-z
book	b-ŏŏ-k	loves	l-ŭ-v-z
good	g-ŏŏ-d	shoves	sh-ŭ-v-z
cook	k-ŏŏ-k	but	b-ŭ-t
push	p-ŏŏ-sh	chum	ch-ŭ-m
nook	n-ŏŏ-k	tub	t-ŭ-b
wool	w-ŏŏ-l	toy	t-oi
full	f-ŏŏ-l	coy	k-oi
rude	r-ū-d	decoy	d-ē-k-oi
view	v-ū	annoy	ă-n-oi
new	n-ū	noise	n-oi-z
jury	j-ū-r-ĭ	voice	v-oi-s
pewter	p-ū-t-ŭ-r	rejoice	r-ē-j-oi-s
duly	d-ū-l-ĭ	enjoy	ĕ-n-j-oi
huge	h-ū-j	point	p-oi-n-t
June	j-ū-n	voyage	v-oi-ā-j
feud	f-ū-d	loiter	l-oi-t-ŭ-r
juice	j-ū-s	doily	d-oi-l-ĭ
up	ŭ-p	now	n-ow

Word.	Elements.	Word.	Elements.
how	h-ow	variety	v-ă-r-ĭ-ĕ-t-ĭ
towel	t-ow-ĕ-l	inform	ĭ-n-f-a̱ r-m
pound	p-ow-n-d	ivory	ĭ-v-ŏ-r-ĭ
downy	d-ow-n-ĭ	purify	p-ū-r-ĭ-f-ĭ
house	h-ow-s	revive	r-ē-v-ĭ-v
cows	k-ow-z	tarry	t-ă-r-ĭ
shout	sh-ow-t	thorough	th-ŭ-r-ŏ
mouth	m-ow-th	sketch	s-k-ĕ-ch
thousand	th-ow-z-ă-n-d	besides	b-ĕ-s-ĭ-d-z
vouch	v-ow-ch	sarcasm	s-ä-r-k-ă-z-m
wound	w-ow-n-d	deposit	d-ē-p-ŏ-z-ĭ-t
thou	th-ow	absence	ă-b-s-ĕ-n-s
know	n-ō	opposite	ŏ-p-ō-z-ĭ-t
bask	b-ä-s-k	welcome	w-ĕ-l-k-ŭ-m
bulky	b-ŭ-l-k-ĭ	witness	w-ĭ-t-n-ĕ-s
office	ŏ-f-ĭ-s	harmony	h-ä-r-m-ō-n-ĭ
opaque	ō-p-ā-k	hammock	h-ă-m-ŏ-k
enough	ē-n-ŭ-f	impeach	ĭ-m-p-ē-ch
namely	n-ā-m-l-ĭ	harangue	h-ă-r-ă-ng
desire	d-ē-z-ĭ-r	hemlock	h-ĕ-m-l-ŏ-k
repose	r-ē-p-ō-z	exercise	ĕ-k-s-ŭ-r-s-ĭ-z
scheme	s-k-ē-m	judgment	j-ŭ-j-m-ĕ-n-t
utmost	ŭ-t-m-ō-s-t	warehouse	w-ā-r-h-ow-s
policy	p-ŏ-l-ĭ-s-ĭ	payments	p-ā-m-ĕ-n-t-s
agency	ā-j-ĕ-n-s-ĭ	certainly	s-ŭ-r-t-ĕ-n-l-ĭ
window	w-ĭ-n-d-ō	amendment	ă-m-ĕ-n-d-m-ĕ-n-t
depth	d-ĕ-p-th	security	s-ē-k-ū-r-ĭ t-ĭ
width	w-ĭ-d-th	citizens	s-ĭ-t-ĭ-z-ĕ-n-z
obtain	ŏ-b-t-ā-n	sufficient	s-ŭ-f-ĭ-sh-ĕ-n-t
secure	s-ē-k-ū-r	unkindness	ŭ-n-k-ĭ-n-d-n-ĕ-s
months	m-ŭ-n-th-s	ignorance	ĭ-g-n-ō-r-ă-n-s
notary	n-ō-t-ā-r-ĭ	arrangement	ă-r-ă-n-j-m-ĕ-n-t

Consonant Alphabet.

7. It has been said that the characters representing these elementary sounds should be the simplest possible, and, therefore, the straight line is used as far as it can be to advantage, as follows:

Phonograph.	Element.	Sound represented.	
		Initial.	Final.
\ represents sound of	P as heard in	pet	and in cap.
\ " "	B " "	bet	" cab.
| " "	T " "	team	" met.
| " "	D " "	deem	" mad.
/ " "	Ch " "	chest	" church.
/ " "	J " "	jest	" page.
— " "	K " "	cane	" took.
▬ " "	G " "	gain	" nag.

8. *K* and *g* (not pronounced as in longhand, but as sounded in the words given above under "Sound represented") are written from left to right, and the other phonographs given above, from top down. The characters should be made the same length as those in this book, one-sixth of an inch, and must be of uniform length. Be specially careful to make *k* and *g* just as long as the other phonographs, and let them rest on the line of writing. *T* and *d* are perpendicular to the base line. Be very careful not to slant them to the right.

9. The best way to memorize the phonographs is to make each one many times, pronouncing the sound represented as you make the corresponding mark. It will be easy to remember which sounds have light phonographs and which heavy, if you observe that the light marks represent light or whispered sounds, and the heavy marks represent heavy

or pronounced sounds. Notice that the position of the vo-
cal organs is the same in pronouncing the sound represented by \ as in that represented by \, the only difference
being that the latter is given more force. There is the
same similarity in each pair of the consonants.

Exercise on Consonants.

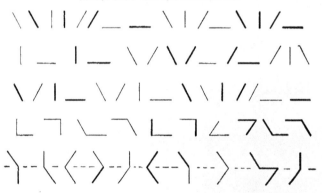

10. The exercise above should first be read aloud by the
student and each character traced with a dry pen or other
point, as its name is pronounced, after which it should be
written several times in the notebook. Pursue the same
course with each of the shorthand exercises that follow.

11. When two or more consonants are joined, the pen
must not be lifted from the paper until the end of the combination is reached. Each consonant must be written in
the same direction as when standing alone.

12. The consonant outline of a word consists of the phonographs which represent the consonant sounds of that word,
made without lifting the pen.

13. An outline composed entirely of horizontal strokes
should rest on the line of writing.

14. An outline composed of one or more horizontals followed by one down stroke should rest on the line.

15. When an outline is composed of two down strokes, the first should rest on the line and the second extend below the line.

16. When two straight consonants are joined, such as *p-p*, *k-k*, *d-d*, they should be made with a single movement of the pen, and double the length of the single stroke.

17. Write carefully the consonant outlines of the following words:

Take, bake, peck, choke, dug, beg, tug, jug, check, catch, pitch, cheap, badge, dog, dodge, page, chalk, keep, cape, judge, duck, batch, depot, peg, pipe, babe, cake, keg, tube, age, gauge, bag, baggage, gape, decay.

18. Having thoroughly mastered the eight straight phonographs, and having learned how to combine them into consonant outlines, the student is ready to learn, in the same way, the following phonographs:

Phonograph.		Element.		Sound represented.		
				Initial.		Final.
	represents sound of	F	as heard in	foam	and in	life.
	" "	V	" "	vine	"	live.
	" "	Th	" "	thigh	"	both.
	" "	th	" "	thy	"	bathe.
	" "	S	" "	seen	"	case.
	" "	Z	" "	zeal	"	cause.
	" "	Sh	" "	shake	"	rush.
	" "	Zh	" "	azure	"	rouge.

19. Each phonograph given above is one-quarter of a circle, and should therefore curve uniformly from beginning to end.

20. The general direction of *f* and *v* is the same as *p*. The general direction of *th, th, s* and *z*, is the same as *t*.   The general direction of *sh* and *zh* is the same as *ch*.

21. By locating each of these curved characters (as well as those given later) on one of the above circles a perfect picture will be formed in the mind's eye, and there will be less danger of making any two of them so that they cannot be distinguished one from the other.

22. All of the above phonographs are *always* made from the top down, except *sh*, which, when standing alone, is always made from top down, but when joined to other strokes is made in the most convenient direction.

23. Read the following exercise carefully, tracing each character with some pointed instrument. Copy same in your notebook.

Exercise on Consonants.

24. Write the consonant outlines of the words given in the following exercise:

Faith, five, fife, tooth, death, fetch, vouch, tithe, ask, espy, above, shabby, shadow, shove, dizzy, veto, shaky, defy, path, both, bathe, sheaf, asp, shape, cash, tissue, depth, fussy, posy.

25. The student will now complete the consonant phonographs by learning the following:

Phonograph.	Element.	Sound represented. Initial. Final.
	represents sound of L as heard in lay and in fail.	
	" " R " " ram " fair.	
	" " R " " ray " tarry.	
	" " M " " make " came.	
	" " N " " neck " seen.	
	" " Ng " " ink " sing.	
	" " W " " way " midway.	
	" " Y " " yes.	
	" " H " " hate.	

26. The second character given in this list is called *downward r* and the third is called *upward r*. Their proper use will be explained later. *Upward r* and *h* are invariably written from bottom up. *L* is always written from bottom up when alone, but when joined to other strokes is sometimes written up and sometimes written down. The horizontal characters, *k, g, m, n*, and *ng*, are written from left to right.

27. The general direction of *l* and *y* is the same as *ch*. The general direction of *downward r* and *w* is the same as *p*.

28. Make the stroke in *h* perfectly straight, and the short line forming the hook at the bottom of *h* should be parallel with the stroke.

29. *Upward r* and *h* should be made at the same angle as the up strokes in the script *m* and *ch* at the same angle as the down strokes in the same letter.   Thus:

30. When standing alone *upward r* is distinguished from *ch* by the slant.   *upward r, / ch.*

31. When joined to other strokes, *upward r* is distinguished from *ch* by the difference in direction, *upward r* being made from bottom up, and *ch*, from top down.

r-p, ch-p, r-n, ch-n.

32. Read the exercise on the following page, tracing each character and observing the following facts: When two characters, extending in the same direction, are joined, they are made with a single motion of the pen.   See lines 1 and 2.   The first up or down stroke rests on the line. See line 3.   There should be an angle between such combinations as *f-n*, *l-m*, etc.   See line 4.   When two consonants do not form a distinct angle, they are so blended that the point of joining cannot be seen. See lines 5 and 6.

33. Copy the exercise on Joined Consonants, next page, several times.   Transcribe the same exercise; that is, write it in longhand. From the transcription, write in shorthand without reference to the book until the whole page has been written.   Compare your characters with those in the book, making the necessary corrections.   Practice the corrected outlines many times.

When the student has mastered all the explanations, and followed all the directions previously given, he may write Exercise No. 1, page 104.

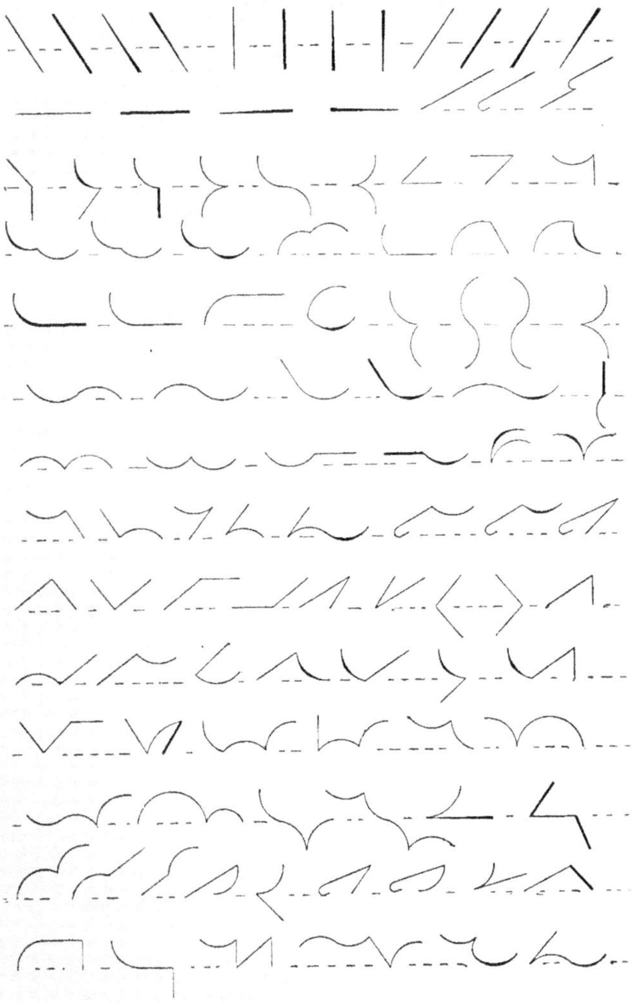

1
2
3
4
5
6
7
8
9
10
11
12
13
14

First Position Vowels.

34. The ordinary alphabet is defective not only in its representation of the consonants, as we have seen, but also in its vowels. The *a, e, i, o, u* scale, is not sufficient to express all the vowel sounds of the English language, and is therefore abandoned and one more complete adopted in its stead.

35. The vowels and diphthongs are divided in shorthand into three classes; namely, first position, second position, and third position. The first position vowels are so called because they are represented by characters placed always at the beginning of some consonant. They are as follows:

ē	a	ĭ	ŏ	ī	oi
eat	thaw	it	odd	die	toy

36. The correct sound of the first heavy dot is heard in *me.* The correct sound of the first heavy dash is heard in *awl.* The correct sound of the first light dot is heard in *it.* The correct sound of the first light dash is heard in *on.* The correct sound of the first angle pointing downward is heard in *my.* The correct sound of the first angle pointing upward is heard in *boy.* Thus, the six first-place vowels occur in regular order in the sentence, " He saw it on my boy."

37. Repeat the above sentence many times, pronouncing each word very carefully. Then pronounce the vowels many times slowly and accurately.

38. Remember that the first-place vowels must be placed at the beginning of all strokes, and will, therefore, always be placed at the bottom of *h* and *upward r*, and at the bottom of *sh* and *l* when they are made from bottom up, and at the left of *k, g, m, n* and *ng.*

39. Dash vowels are written at right angles to the stroke but should not touch it. When good angles would result, *i* and *oi* may be joined to the beginning of a stroke, as in ⟍ *ivy*, ⟋ *oil*.

40. It must be constantly kept in mind that these vowels do not represent longhand letters, but sounds, and each vowel always the same sound; thus, the first heavy dot stands for long *e*, as heard in *beat*, but not for the short vowel sound as heard in *bet*. ⌄ stands for long *i*, as heard in *mile*, but the vowel in *mill* is the first light dot.

41. The order of reading is the natural order; namely, all uprights from left to right, and all horizontals from top down. Thus, a vowel placed at the left of *t* is to be read before the *t*, and a vowel at the right of *t*, after it. Therefore, | represents *e-t* (*eat*), and | represents *t-e* (*tea*); ⋅__ represents *e-k* (*eke*) and ⌐__ represents *k-e* (*key*).

42. Outlines of all words containing first position vowels are written in the first position. The first position for upright outlines is half a stroke above the line of writing, and for horizontal outlines a stroke above the line. If an outline contains more than one upright consonant, the first up or down stroke takes position.

43. When first-place vowels come between two strokes they are placed after the first stroke.

44. All the consonants of a word are written first and the vowels inserted afterwards.

Read from the next page the words containing first position vowels. Transcribe same. From the transcription, write in shorthand. Compare and correct. Re-write the words with which you made errors. Re-write the entire page, and again correct. Continue writing from the longhand and comparing with the engraved page until you can write the entire page without an error.

Write Exercise No. 2, page 104.

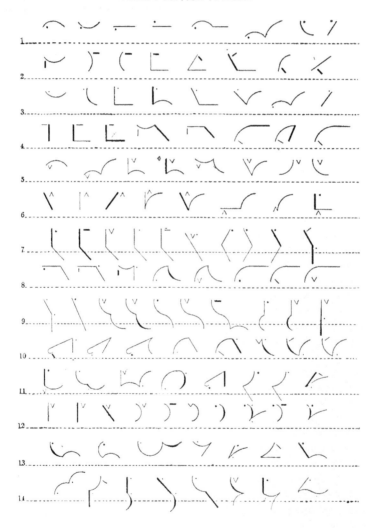

Second Position Vowels.

45. There are four second-place vowels. They are represented by dots and dashes placed at the middle of some
consonant, and are as follows:

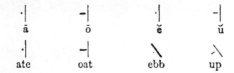

46. The correct sound of the second heavy dot is heard
in *may*. The correct sound of the second heavy dash is
heard in *go*. The correct sound of the second light dot is
heard in *ebb*. The correct sound of the second light dash
is heard in *up*. These four second-place vowels occur in
regular order in the following sentence: "They go yet
up."

47. Repeat the above sentence many times, pronouncing
each word very carefully. Then pronounce the vowels
many times, slowly and carefully.

48. When second-place vowels come between two strokes,
the long ones, ā and ō are placed *after the first stroke*, and
the short ones ĕ and ŭ are placed *before the second stroke*.

49. All words containing second-place vowels are written
in the second position that is, resting on the line of
writing. Words containing vowels of different positions
should be put in the position of the accented vowel. See
lines 10 and 11.

The method of practice for the next page should be the
same as that given for the first position vowels.

Write Exercise No. 3, page 105.

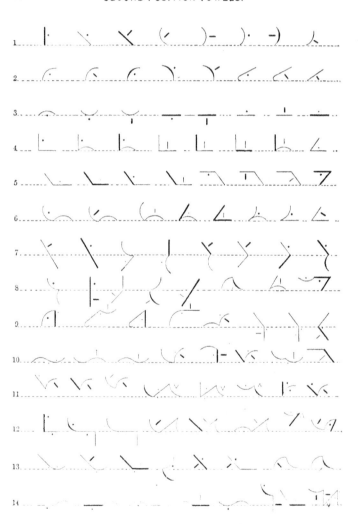

Third Position Vowels.

50. There are six third-place vowels. They are represented by characters placed at the end of some consonant, and are as follows :

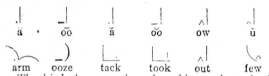

ä	·	ōō	ă	ŏŏ	ow	ŭ
arm	ooze	tack	took	out	few

51. The third-place vowels are heard in regular order in the following sentence : "Arthur, move that book round you."

52. Repeat the above sentence many times, pronouncing each word very carefully. Then pronounce the vowels many times slowly and accurately.

53. When third-place vowels come between two strokes, they are placed *before the second* so as to keep the vowel out of the angle. ⟍⟋ *balm*, not ⟍⟍, because this might be read *beam*.

54. All words containing third-place vowels are written in the third position ; namely, through the line for uprights, and under the line for horizontals.

55. Forty sounds (twenty-four consonant and sixteen vowel) have now been brought to the student's attention, and a sign given to represent each. These sounds should be repeatedly pronounced, until any word in the language can be separated into its elementary sounds. Every word as it falls upon the ear must be analyzed before it can be written in shorthand. It will be found excellent practice to thus analyze any words seen in print or heard in conversation. The exercise on analysis of words, pages 2–6, should now be reviewed.

Practice the engraved page in the same manner as directed for first and second position vowels. Write Exercise No. 4, page 105.

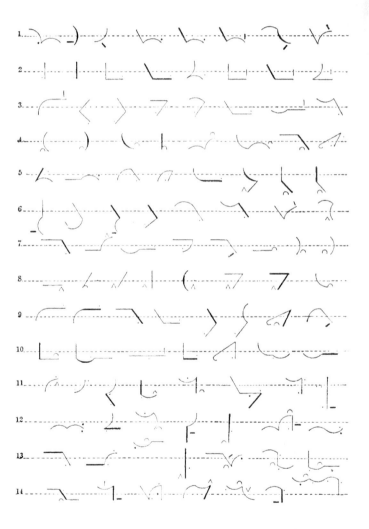

Use of Upward and Downward R.

56. The sound represented by *upward r* is the same as that represented by the *downward r*, and it is not, therefore, the *sound* of a word that determines which one shall be used.

57. There are two things upon which the use of *upward* and *downward r* depend; namely, the angle at the joining with other strokes, and the vowel.

58. In order to secure good angles the following rules should be observed: —

I. Use *downward r* before *m:* ⟍⌢ See line 1, page 23.

II. Use *upward r* before *t, d, ch, j, f, v, th, th, n,* or *ng :* See line 2, page 23.

III. Use *upward r* after *upward r* or *m.* See line 3, page 23.

59. In reading shorthand in which the vowels are not inserted (explained hereafter) great assistance is derived from the observation of the following rules: —

I. When a word begins with the sound of *r*, use *upward r.* *rope,* *write.* See line 4.

II. When a word begins with a vowel sound followed by *r*, use *downward r.* *ark,* *herb.* See line 5.

III. When a word ends with the sound of *r*, use *downward r.* *par,* *tore.* See line 7.

IV. When a word ends with a vowel sound preceded by *r*, use *upward r,* *berry,* *tarry.* See line 8.

These last four rules are to be applied in all cases where they do not clash with the three given above them.

Use of Upward and Downward L.

60. *L* should be made from the top down in the following cases: —

I. When a word begins with a vowel followed by *l-k*, *l-g*, *l-m*, *l-n*, or *l-ng*. See line 13.

II. When a word ends with the sound of *l*, and the consonant preceding it is *f*, *v*, or *upward r*. See line 14.

III. After *n* or *ng* : ⌐ *nail*, ⌐ *Nellie*, ⌐ *wrongly*.

61. When *l* is the only stroke in the outline, and in all cases not mentioned in the above three rules, make *l* from bottom up. One other direction with regard to *l* will be given in Par. 73.

Practice the following page in the manner directed for previous engraved pages, after which write Exercise No. 5, page 107.

Review Exercises.

1. What should the characters of an alphabet represent?
2. How should the characters be assigned to the sounds?
3. Are these things true of the longhand alphabet now in use?
4. Give some examples of ridiculous spelling as used in longhand.
5. How are words spelled in shorthand?
6. What is a consonant outline?
7. In what direction is *sh* written when standing alone?
8. In what direction is *l* written when standing alone?
9. How are *h* and *upward r* written?
10. How are the horizontal characters written?
11. What caution is given with regard to *h*?
12. How can *upward r* be distinguished from *ch* when standing alone?
13. How can *upward r* be distinguished from *ch* when joined to other strokes?
14. Give the sounds of the consonants used in shorthand.

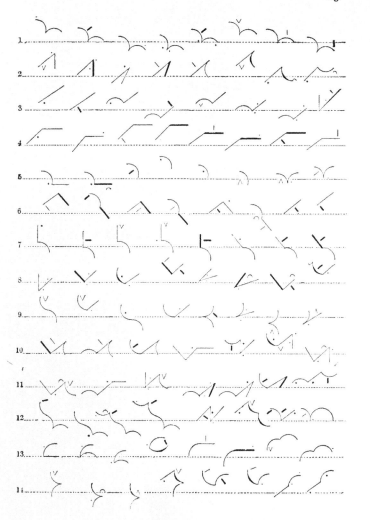

Circle S and Z.

62. As has been said, frequently recurring sounds must be represented in shorthand by easily formed characters.

63. *S* and *z* are sounds that occur more frequently than any other pair. They must, therefore, be represented by the easiest possible mark — a small circle.

64. This circle may be joined at the beginning or end of any stroke. When used at the beginning of an outline it always represents the sound of *s*. When used at the end of an outline it represents the sound of either *s* or *z*.

65. When the circle begins an outline it is read first. *side.* See lines 3 and 4.

66. When the circle ends an outline it is read last. *does.* See line 2.

67. The writer should constantly bear in mind that it is the stroke which he vocalizes, and place the vowel on the same side of the stroke that he would if no circle were attached. Thus:—

eat, up, oak, aim, ale, oar, seat, sup, soak, same, sale, soar.

68. When a circle is attached to a single stroke, either at the beginning or at the end, it is written as follows:—

I. On the right side of down straight strokes.

II. On the left side of up straight strokes.

III. On the upper side of horizontal straight strokes.

IV. On the inside of curves.

69. When the circle comes between two strokes it is written as follows:—   [line 7.

I. Between two straight strokes, outside the angle. See

II. Between a straight stroke and a curve, inside the curve. See line 8.

III. Between two curves, generally inside the first curve.

mason.   (Continued on page 26.)

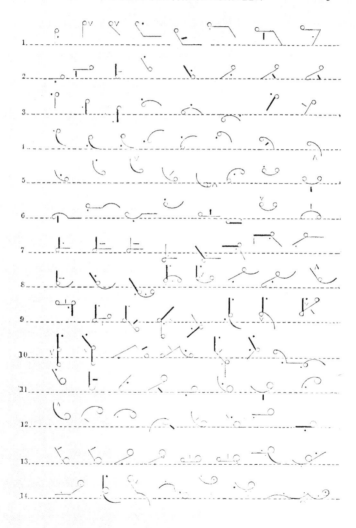

Circle Sez.

70. The circle may be made double its usual size to represent two sounds of *s* or *z*, as follows: *ses, sez, zes, zez.* These sounds are heard in the following words, *recess, cases, possess, roses.* See line 11.

71. The circle *s* may be added to the *sez* circle. See line 13.

72. When no vowel is written within the *sez* circle, the vowel *é* is understood; but any other vowel may be expressed by inserting the desired vowel within the circle. See line 14.

73. When *l* comes before *s-n* make the *l* downward. *lesson.* (Refer to Par. 61.)

After practicing the engraved page in the usual manner, write Exercise No. 6, page 107.

Review Exercises.

15. How are the vowels and diphthongs divided in shorthand?

16. Why are first-place vowels so called?

17. Give the sounds of the first-place vowels. Give the sentence containing them in regular order.

18. At which end of a consonant are first-place vowels always written?

19. How are dash vowels written with reference to the stroke to which they are placed?

20. At which side of an upright stroke must a vowel be placed to have the vowel read first?

21. At which side of a horizontal stroke must a vowel be placed to have the vowel read first?

22. In what position should the outline of a word containing a first-place vowel be written?
23. What is the first position for outlines containing upright strokes?
24. What is the first position for outlines composed of horizontal strokes?
25. Give the sounds of the second-place vowels. Give the sentence containing them in regular order.
26. In what position should the outline of a word containing a second-place vowel be written?
27. What is the second position?
28. What determines the position of words containing vowels of two different positions?
29. Give the sounds of the third-place vowels. Give the sentence containing them in regular order.
30. In what position should the outline of a word containing a third-place vowel be written?
31. What is the third position for outlines containing upright strokes?
32. What is the third position for outlines composed of horizontal strokes?
33. How many elementary sounds are represented in shorthand?
34. Give all the consonant sounds. Give all the vowel sounds.
35. Upon what two things does the use of upward and downward s depend?
36. Give the rules depending upon the angle.
37. Give the rules depending upon the vowel.
38. Give the rules for upward and downward l.
39. What pair of outlines stands oftener more frequently than any other?
40. What is the contraction for out?
41. When the small circle is used at the beginning of an outline which is represented by hand, how is it read?

Loops st, zd, str.

74. The consonants *s* and *t* occur frequently without a vowel between the *s* and *t*, and in such cases may be represented by a small loop one-half the length of the stroke to which it is attached. The loop should be very narrow.

75. The *st* loop is written on the same side of the different strokes as the circles *s* and *sez;* namely, right side of down straight strokes, left side of up straight strokes, upper side of horizontal straight strokes, and inside of curves.

76. An outline containing a loop is vocalized and read in the same manner as one containing a circle; that is, the vowel is placed and read with reference to the stroke, and if the loop begins the outline it is read before every thing, and if it ends the outline it is read after every thing. See line 5.

77. The small loop may also be used to represent *zd*. See line 8.

78. The *st* loop may also, when convenient, be written in the middle of an outline. See line 9. But the following stroke must not cut through the one to which the loop is attached.

79. A large loop extending about two-thirds the length of the stroke to which it is attached, placed upon the same side as the *st* loop, and vocalized and read like it, represents the sounds *str*.

80. The loop *str* is used only at the end of outlines.

81. The circle *s* may follow either the *st* or the *str* loop. See line 11.

82. Be careful to make the *st* loop very thin and the *str* loop wider, in order that they may be distinguished.

Prepare the lesson in the usual manner and write Exercise No. 7, page 108.

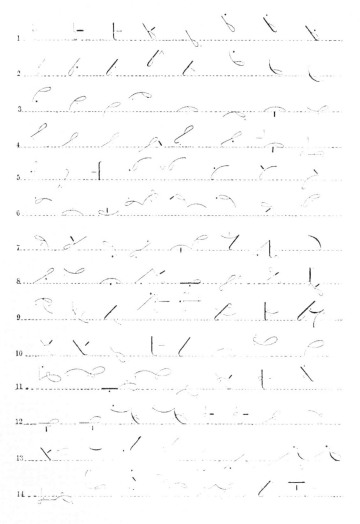

When to Use Circles and Loops.

83. Since the circles and loops not only increase the speed in writing shorthand, but add to its legibility, we, of course, use them whenever possible. We have, therefore, only to learn the cases where we *cannot* use them.

84. As it is impossible to vocalize circle *s*, whenever a vowel is placed to *s*, we must use the stroke; hence the following

Rules for the Use of Stroke S.

a. When a word begins with a vowel immediately followed by *s*, use the stroke. (Line 1.)

b. When a word ends with a vowel immediately preceded by *s*, use the stroke. (Line 2.)

c. When there are two necessary vowels between *s* and a preceding or following consonant, use the stroke. See line 5.

85. The rules for the use of the circle representing the sound of *z* are the same as for *s*, except that when a word begins with the sound of *z* we use the stroke. See line 6. There are two reasons for using the stroke *z* at the beginning of words; first, because so few words begin with the sound of *z* that it is not necessary to use the more contracted form, and second, because words of rare occurrence are not easily read unless very fully written.

86. The loop for *st* cannot be used when the word ends with a vowel preceded by *st*, nor when there is a vowel between the *s* and *t*. See line 7.

Do not neglect to practice the next page in the following manner. 1. Read. 2. Copy. 3. Transcribe. 4. Write from transcript. 5. Correct. 6. Read from your own writing. Repeat 4, 5, and 6 many times or until there are no corrections to be made and until you can both write and read without hesitation. Write Exercise No. 8, page 108.

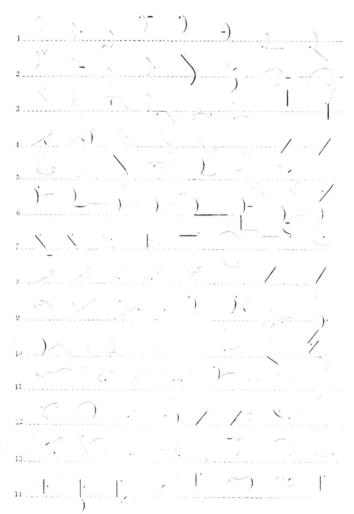

The Initial W Hook.

87. A small hook written at the beginning of *l, upward r, m,* and *n,* represents *w,* and it is written on the inside of

the three curves,   ⌒ wl,   ⌒ wm,   ⌣ wn,

and on the left-hand side of *upward r,* ╱ wr.

88. The initial hook *w,* like the initial circle *s,* is read first and the vowels are placed and read with reference to the stroke.

89. The circle *s* may be written within the *w* hook, as follows :

   ⌀ swl,   swr,   swm,   swn.

90. When the circle is written within the hook, the circle should be commenced in the same direction as the beginning of the stroke to which the hook and circle are attached.

91. The sound of *h* need not be represented when it

comes before the *w* hook. *Weal* and *wheel* are written

and are readily distinguished by the context. See line 5.

92. The student will observe that the first sound in *wheel, when, whim, where,* and, in fact, all words that in longhand commence with *wh,* is *h.*

93. *W,* before all strokes, except *l, upward r, m,* and *n,* is written with a semicircle curving either to the left or right.

94. Use the semicircle curving to the left, providing it makes a good angle with the following stroke (see line 6); if not, use the one curving to the right. See line 7. Before *k, g* or *ng,* the semicircle *w* must always curve to the right, thus : ⌣ *w-k,* ⌣ *w-g,* ⌣ *w-ng.*

95. A semicircle curving upward or downward may be used to represent the sound of *y.* See line 8. Use whichever semicircle makes the better angle.

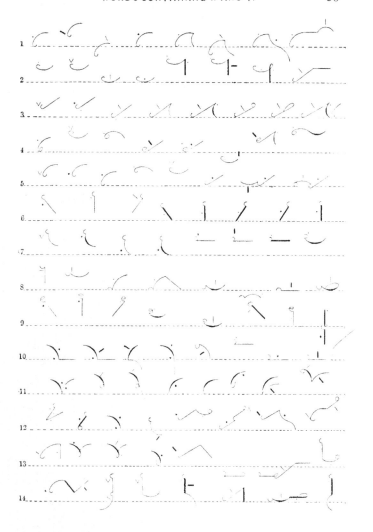

96. The circle *s* may be written within the semicircles. See line 9.

97. When a word begins with a vowel followed by *w* or *y*, the strokes must be used.   See line 10.

98. When the stroke is more conveniently written, or makes a more suggestive outline, it should be used in preference to the semicircle.   See line 11.

99. Make the semicircles very small ; not more than one-quarter the length of a stroke.

100. Make the initial *w* hook small, and do not allow the beginning of the hook to curve in toward the stroke or it may be mistaken for the circle *s*.

Practice page 33 as usual. Write Exercise No. 9, page 110.

Heavy M.

101. *M* may be made heavy to represent the sound of *mp* (see line 1) or *mb*.   See line 2.

102. The heavy *m* represents *mp* much more frequently than *mb*, and, therefore, in reading, *mp* should always be tried first.   If that does not give the word, try *mb*.

Tick H.

103. A short tick made in the direction of *ch* (always down) and one-quarter as long as *ch*, represents *h*.   See line 5.

104. It, however, can only be used to advantage before the following strokes: *k, g, m, mp, downward r, w, l, p, b, s* and *z*.

105. The tick *h* at the beginning of an outline is read first.

106. The tick *h* may be used in the middle of an outline if it makes a good angle with both the preceding and following stroke.

107. In a few words of frequent occurrence *h* may be omitted.   See line 11.

Apply directions given at bottom of page 30 to the exercise on the next page. Write Exercise No. 10, page 110.

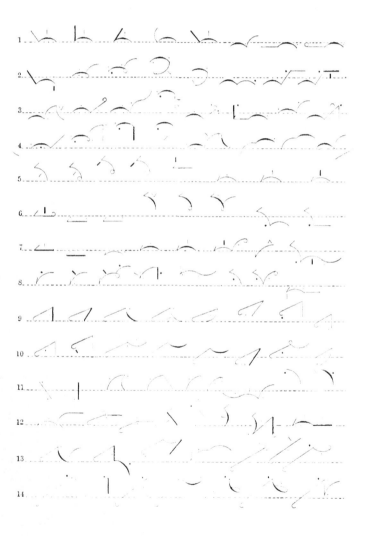

Review Exercises.

42. When the small circle is used at the end of an outline, what is represented by it, and how is it read?
43. Can the circle be vocalized?
44. On which side of a single straight stroke is the circle written? On which side of a curve?
45. How is the circle written when it comes between two strokes?
46. What sounds are represented by the large circle?
47. What is represented by a small loop?
48. When the *st* loop is written in the middle of an outline, how must the following stroke be made?
49. What is represented by a large loop?
50. When must the stroke be used for *s?*
51. When must the stroke be used for *z?*
52. To what strokes is the initial *w* hook attached?
53. What may be written within the *w* hook?
54. When a circle is written within a hook how should the circle be commenced?
55. What is the first sound in such words as *when, whim,* and *where?*
56. What contraction is used for *w* when it occurs before strokes other than *l, r, m,* and *n?*
57. What contraction represents the sound of *y?*
58. When should the strokes for *w* and *y* be used?
59. What is represented by heavy *m?*
60. Which occurs the more frequently?
61. Describe the tick *h.*
62. Before what strokes is the tick *h* used?

Word-Signs.

108. Some words occur much more frequently than others. In fact, one-half of any subject-matter is made up of less than two hundred words frequently repeated.

109. These very frequently occurring words must be represented by very easily formed characters. A single motion of the pen must be made, as far as possible, to represent a complete word.

110. When a part only of an outline is used to represent the whole word, or when a short outline is confined to some other position than that of the vowel in the word, it is called a word-sign.

111. The word-signs must be thoroughly learned and repeatedly reviewed.

112. The student will notice in the following list of word-signs, and in all lists given hereafter, that the character used represents a prominent sound in the word and is suggestive of the whole word. They are not arbitrary signs.

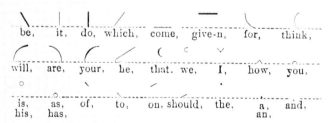

be, it, do, which, come, give-n, for, think,

will, are, your, he, that. we, I, how, you,

is, as, of, to, on, should, the, a, and,
his, has, an,

113. Be careful always to keep the word-signs in the positions in which they are here given.

114. The word-signs *on* and *should* are made from bottom up.

115. Two or more words may be written without lifting the pen, providing the joinings are good and there is no natural pause between them. Words thus united are called

Phrases.

of-the,   to-the,   to-you,   you-should,   you-may,

if-you,   you-will,   of-it,   of-your,   it-will-be,

116. In phrasing, a short tick made in the direction of *ch* or *upward r* may be used to represent *the*, and in the direction of *t* or *k* to represent *a*, *an*, or *and*.

117. In learning the word-signs and phrases, a good plan is to write the words and phrases in a column at the left margin of a sheet of practice paper, and then fill out each line by writing the words over and over, being very careful each time to write them correctly, and to think of the word or phrase represented.

118. The sentences given in connection with each list of word-signs should first be read over two or three times, after which they should be copied slowly and accurately. Next, make a longhand copy of the page, from which write in shorthand and compare with the book.   Read your own notes. Write, compare, and read repeatedly until you make no mistakes in writing, and can read your notes as readily as a printed page.

119. *Always* carry in your pocket a list of words to study at leisure moments.

The period is represented by a cross on the line and the question mark by the same character above the line, as shown at the end of sentences on page 39.

Write Exercise No. 11, page 111.

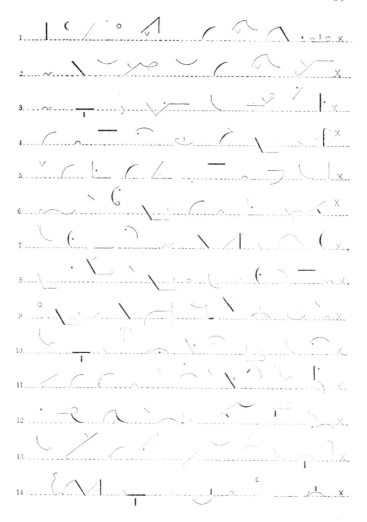

Word-Signs and Phrases.

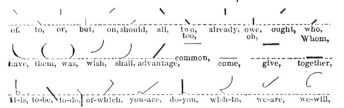

of, to, or, but, on, should, all, two, too, already, owe, oh, ought, who, Whom,

have, them, was, wish, shall, advantage, common, come, give, together,

it-is, to-be, to-do, of-which, you-are, do-you, wish-to, we-are, we-will,

120. Where the same mark represents two word-signs, the only difference being in position, the words should be fixed in the mind in a regular order.

Example :—*given, together ; wish, shall ; common, come.*

121. The words represented by the dash vowels in the different positions should be memorized in regular order, thus :—

Of, to, or, but, on, should. All, two, already, owe, ought, who.

122. While for most beginners a pencil will be found more convenient, the student should, early in his practice, accustom himself to the use of a pen. It is recommended that, from this point on, the student use a pen in at least a part of his practice. An ordinary steel pen may be used, or, better, a good gold pen, either fountain or otherwise. When pencils are used, they should be of good quality and several, well-sharpened, should always be at hand. In selecting either pen or pencil, the student should be careful to obtain one suited to his particular touch, and then always use the same kind.

In studying this list of word-signs, follow the directions given in sections 117 and 118.

Write Exercise No. 12, page 111.

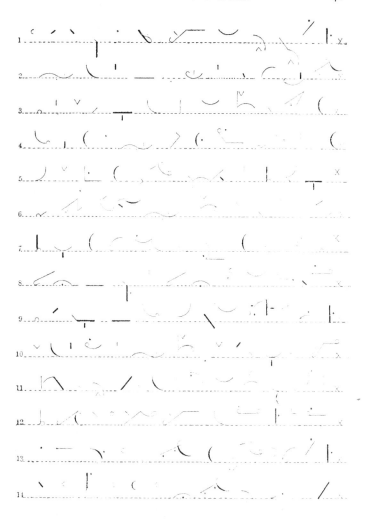

Word-Signs and Phrases.

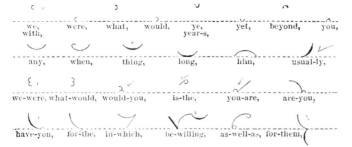

123. It will be observed that the words given in the first half of the first line in this group of word-signs, begin with *w* and they are, therefore, very properly represented by the *w* semicircle. It will also be seen that the words in the last half of the same line contain *y* as a prominent sound and are represented by the *y* semicircle. These semicircles should be made very small; if made too large, they will clash with the half-lengths given later.

124. After this list of word-signs has been learned the two previous lists should be reviewed and each word practiced many hundred times. A great deal of trouble will be prevented by thoroughly learning the word-signs as they are given, and by repeatedly reviewing them.

Apply the directions given in paragraphs 117 and 118 to this lesson. Write Exercise No. 13, page **112.**

Straight Double Consonants.

125. We have in our English language many sounds of *l* and *r* immediately after, and closely uniting with, other consonants. These combined sounds may be heard at the beginning of such words as *play, pray, black, brick, clay, crow, tree, try,* etc.

(Continued on page 44)

126. The eight straight consonants *p, b, t, d, ch, j, k, g,* are changed to double consonants in the following simple way : —

\	\	ſ	ſ	/	/	⌐	⌐
pl,	bl,	tl,	dl,	chl,	jl,	kl,	gl,

\	\	˥	˥	/	/	⌐	⌐
pr,	br,	tr,	dr,	chr,	jr,	kr,	gr,

127. The stroke and the hook must not be construed as representing each a separate consonant, but each sign is an indivisible compound, representing the double consonants *pl, pr,* etc.

128. In naming the characters of the double consonant series, it is best to call them by single syllables. Thus, ˥ is *tr*, as heard in *utter*, not *t-r ;* \ *pr*, as heard in *upper*, not *p-r;* \ *pl*, as heard in *apple*, not *p l*. This remark applies to all the characters of the *pl* and *pr* series.

129. The double consonant sounds are not to be used when a distinct accented vowel comes between two letters, as in the words *tear* and *tool*, but should be employed when the *l* or *r* follows immediately after the other consonant, as in *tree, try, play*, etc., and also when the vowel sound is obscure and unaccented, as in lines 6 to 14.

130. The double consonants are vocalized the same as the single consonants ; that is, any vowel placed at the left of uprights or above horizontals is read before the double consonant, and any vowel placed at the right of uprights or below horizontals is read after the double consonant.

131. When the *l* and *r* hooks appear in the middle of outlines it is sometimes impossible to form them perfectly, and, in such cases, they may be made by retracing the previous stroke. See lines 10 and 11.

132. Be careful not to make the hooks too large, and do not make them look like circles. Try to make your double consonants just like those in the exercises.

Practice the exercise on the next page in the usual manner.

Write Exercise No. 14, page 114.

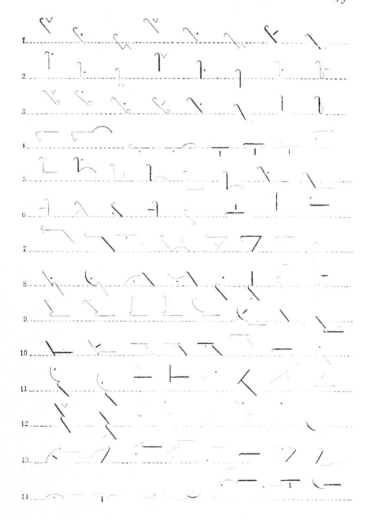

Curved Double Consonants.

133. It is not possible to form double consonants with all the curved strokes, because all the hooks attached to curves must be on the inside of the curve. Neither is it necessary, because some consonants are never immediately followed by *l* or *r*.

134. The curved double consonants are as follows:

fl, vl, thl, thl, shl, zhl,

fr, vr, thr, thr, shr, zhr,

mr, nr,

135. It will be seen in the above list of double conso-nants that *fl, vl, thl,* and *thl* are formed just as the straight double consonants are formed; namely, by placing the hook at the beginning on the right-hand side, and that these characters are inverted to represent *fr, vr, thr,* and *thr.* This is, in reality, precisely what is done with the straight consonants, for if *pl* were made of wire and then turned over, it would give *pr ;* thus, *pl* ⟍ *pr ; fl* ⟍ *fr.*

136. It will also be seen that *shr* and *zhr* are formed by a hook on the left-hand side in the regular way, and that they are inverted *endwise* instead of sidewise to produce the double consonants *shl* and *zhl.*

137. *Shr* and *zhr* must always be made from the top down.

138. *Shl* and *zhl* are always made from bottom up, and must never stand alone.

139. *Mr* and *nr* must be shaded to distinguish them from *w-m* and *w-n.*

140. Do not allow the hooks on the curved strokes to bend in toward the stroke too much, because in such case they are likely to be mistaken for the circle *s.*

141. The double curved consonants are read and vocal-ized the same as the double straight consonants, and their names are similar, being *fl,* as heard in *muffle ; fr,* as heard in *offer,* etc.

Pursue the usual method of practice. Write Exercise No. 15, page 114.

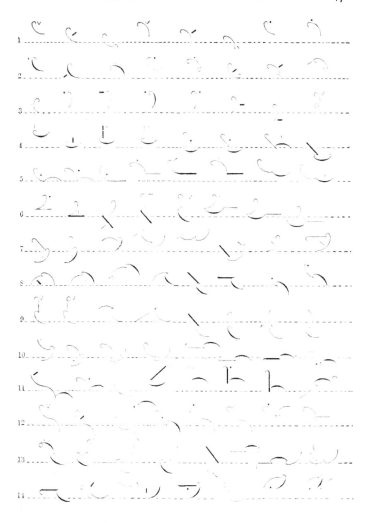

The Triple Consonants.

142. When *s* comes before the double consonants, a series of triple consonants is formed, as heard in the words *spray, stray, splash*, etc.

143. When *s* comes before a straight double consonant of the *pr* series, the triple consonant is expressed by putting the circle *in place of the hook*, thus :—

spr,	sbr,	str,	sdr,	schr,	sjr,	skr,	sgr,

144. A vowel placed at the right of a triple consonant is read after the triple consonant, Example, *stray*.

145. Any vowel placed at the left of a triple consonant is read between the *s* and the stroke, in accordance with the rules already given for circle *s*. Example, *cider*.

146. When *s* comes before straight double consonants of the *pl* series, the triple consonant is expressed by placing the circle *within the hook*, thus :—

spl,	sbl,	stl,	sdl,	schl,	sjl,	skl,	sgl,

147. When the *s* comes before any curved double consonant it is written inside the hook. Always start a circle within a hook in the direction in which the stroke to which they are attached commences.

148. When triple consonants (whether straight or curved) occur after other strokes, the circle must, if possible, show within the hook. See line 7.

149. If it is impossible to write the circle within the hook, then the circle must be flattened as in line 9.

(*Continued on page* 50.)

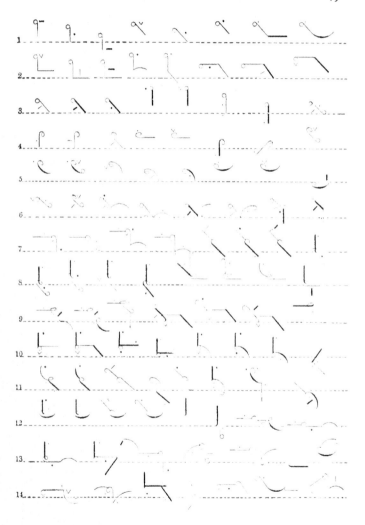

150. When *skr*, *sgr*, *sfr*, or *svr* follow *T* or *D*, and when *spr* follows *J*, the circle should be placed on the *s* side of the first stroke and the *r* side of the second stroke, as follows: See line 10, page 49.

151. The circle *sez* may also be written on the left side at the beginning of straight strokes to represent *sez* before a double consonant, as in *sister*.

After studying and practicing this lesson in the usual manner, write Exercise No. 16, page 115.

The N Hook.

152. A small hook may be written at the end of any stroke consonant to represent the sound of *n*.

153. This hook is placed on the left-hand side of down straight strokes, the right-hand side of up straight strokes, the under side of horizontal straight strokes, and inside of all curves.

154. The *n* hook, like the circle *s*, is always read last when it ends an outline. A vowel may, and in fact almost always does, come between the stroke and the *n*.

155. The *n* hook may be used in the middle of an outline, as in lines 12 and 13.

156. When a word ends with a vowel preceded by *n*, it is necessary to use the stroke for *n*. See line 14.

157. The *n* hook, like all the appendages (circles, hooks, loops, etc.), is not only valuable because it increases speed in writing, but because it adds to the legibility of the notes. Thus, a hook *n* at the end of an outline indicates that the word ends with the sound of *n*, and a stroke *n* at the end of an outline usually indicates a final vowel. Study and practice this lesson as usual after which, write Exercise No. 17, page 116.

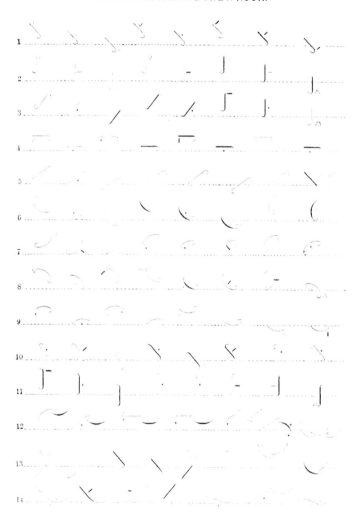

The F or V Hook.

158. The f or v hook may be attached at the end of any straight stroke, but cannot be attached to curves.

159. The hook for f or v is written on the same side as circle s; namely, the right side of down strokes, left side of up strokes, upper side of horizontal strokes.

160. The hook f or v is read just like circle s and hook n; that is, always last when it ends an outline.

161. When a word ends with a vowel immediately preceded by f or v, the stroke must be used for f or v. Therefore, hook f or v at the end of an outline indicates that the word ends with the sound of f or v, but stroke f or v at the end of an outline indicates that the word ends with a vowel. Example, ╱ *roof*; ╱╲ *review*.

162. The hook f or v may be frequently used in the middle of an outline. See line 5.

S Added to the Final Hooks.

163. The circle s may be written within the f or v hook, and is then read after every thing, as circle s, at the end of an outline, is always read last.

164. The circles s and sez and the loops st and str may be written in place of the n hook on straight strokes to add that which is expressed by the circle or loop to that which is expressed by the hook; thus: —

     ↓ tns,   ↓ tnsez,   ↓ tnst,   ↓ tnstr,

165. Circle s may be written within an n hook on curves, but when sez, st, or str follows n after curves, the stroke n must be used. Example, ╲╱ *fences*.

166. The n hook followed by circle s may sometimes be used in the middle of a word, but the circle must always show distinctly within the hook. See line 12.

Write Exercise No. 18, page 117.

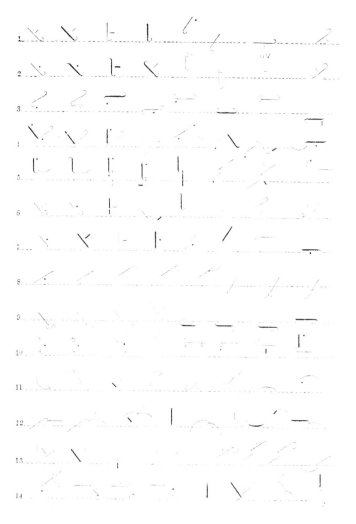

Double Consonant Word-Signs.

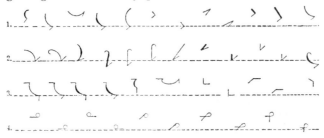

principal-ly principle	practice	member remember-ed	number-ed	truth

doctor	dear	during	tell till	until

care	call	difficult-y	Mr. remark-able	more

near nor	full-y	from	every very	value

three	there their	other	sure-ly	pleasure

The following phrases are written in accordance with paragraph 116. The same will be found in print at the beginning of Exercise 19, page 117.

167. Do not make the ticks too long; they should not exceed one-quarter the length of a stroke consonant.

168. Always use the tick which forms the better angle with the stroke to which it is attached. When good angles do not result by the use of the ticks, the dots must be used for *a, an, and,* and *the,* as given in the first list of word-signs. Write Exercise No. 19, page 117.

Review Exercises.

63. What is a word-sign?
64. Are the word-signs arbitrary marks?
65. When may two or more words be joined?
66. What are such joined words called?
67. How is *the* represented in phrasing?
68. How is *a, an,* or *and* represented in phrasing?
69. What are formed when the sound of *l* or *r* combines with other consonant sounds?
70. Name the straight double consonants of the *pl* series.
71. Name the straight double consonants of the *pr* series.
72. How are the double consonants vocalized?
73. Is it possible to form double consonants with all the curved strokes?
74. Name the curved double consonants of the *fl* series.
75. Name the curved double consonants of the *fr* series.
76. Why are *mr* and *nr* made heavy?
77. In what direction should *shr* and *zhr* be made?
78. In what direction should *shl* and *zhl* be made?
79. How are double consonants of the *pr* series changed to triple consonants?
80. How are double consonants of the *pl* series changed to triple consonants?
81. How are the curved double consonants changed to triple consonants?
82. How may the triple consonants be vocalized?
83. When triple consonants come after other strokes how should they be made?
84. How are *skr, sgr, sfr,* and *svr* written after *t* or *d?*
85. Upon which side of straight strokes is the *n* hook written? Upon which side of curves?
86. How is the *n* hook read when it ends an outline?
87. If a word ends with a vowel sound preceded by *n,* how must the *n* be written?

88. How does the *n* hook add to the legibility of short-hand notes?

89. To what strokes may the *f* or *v* hook be attached?

90. On which side is the *f* or *v* hook written?

91. What is indicated by the use of hook *f* or *v* at the end of an outline? What by the use of stroke *f* or *v*?

92. How is circle *s* added to the *f* or *v* hook?

93. How are the circles and loops added to the *n* hook following straight strokes?

94. How is the circle *s* added to the *n* hook on curves?

95. When hook and circle are used together in the middle of a word, how must they be written?

The Large Wa Hook.

169. The sound of *w* frequently follows *t*, *d*, *k*, and *g*, and coalesces with them in a manner similar to *l* and *r* in the double consonant sounds already given.

170. These combined sounds of *tw*, *dw*, *kw*, *gw*, are represented by a large initial hook on the circle *s* side of the stroke, thus:—

⎰ tw, ⎰ dw, ⌒ kw, ⌒ gw,

171. These sounds are heard in the words *twig*, *dwell*, *quill*, *anguish*, etc., and may be spoken of as *twa*, *dwa*, *kwa*, and *gwa*.

The Large Wa Hook — Continued.

172. Students sometimes find it difficult to analyze words which in longhand are spelled with the letters *qu ;* as, *quick, queen,* etc.   It will be observed, upon carefully pronouncing such words, that the sounds represented by these letters are really *kw.*

173. These signs are vocalized the same as the double consonants (see paragraph 130); that is, the vowel may come either before or after the combined sound, but never between the stroke and the hook.

174. The circle *s* may be written within the *w* hook, and is then read and vocalized the same as the triple consonants.   See paragraphs 144 and 149.   See line 6.

175. When the word ends with the sound of *L* after *Kw* it should be made from top downward.   See beginning of line 5.

Ml, Nl, Rl, and Lr.

176. A large hook at the beginning of *m, n* and *upward r,* adds *l,* and at the beginning of *l,* adds *r ;* thus : —

$$\frown \text{ ml,} \qquad \smile \text{ nl,} \qquad \diagup \text{ rl,} \qquad (\text{ lr,}$$

177. These are double consonants and are read and vocalized in accordance with the rules for double consonants given in paragraph 130.

178. Care must be exercised in writing this series to make the hook large, in order that it may be distinguished from the small initial *w* hook, explained in paragraph 87.

179. It will occasionally be convenient and also safe, especially in long outlines, to use *ml, nl, rl,* and *lr,* even when there is a vowel between.   See line 14.

Write Exercise No. 20, page 120.

LARGE INITIAL HOOKS.

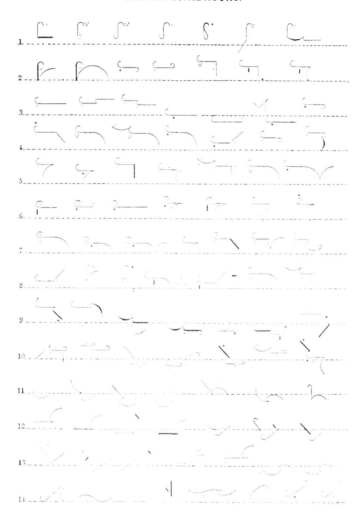

The Large Final Hooks.

180. A large final hook on the circle *s* side (paragraph 68) of any stroke, adds the sound of *shun* or *zhun*.

181. A vowel may come before the stroke or between the stroke and the hook, the same as the other final hooks.

182. A large final hook on the opposite side of straight strokes adds the sound of *ther*, *ter*, or *der*, and is vocalized the same as the *shun* hook given above.

183. Circle *s* may be added to either of these hooks by placing the circle within the hook.

The S-shun Curl.

184. When the sound of *shun* follows circle *s* or *ns*, it is represented by continuing the line of the circle through to the opposite side of the stroke. See lines 8 and 9.

185. This is called the *s-shun* curl, and may be vocalized for a first or second-place vowel as follows: A first-place vowel coming between *s* and *shun* is placed before and near the end of the stroke to which the *s-shun* curl is attached; and a second-place vowel coming between *s* and *shun* is placed after, and near the end of the stroke to which the *s-shun* curl is attached.

186. Third-place vowels never come between *s* and *shun*.

187. Circle *s* may be added to the *s-shun* curl as in line 10.

188. When *sh* and *n* are the only consonant sounds in a word, the stroke *sh* and the hook *n* must be used, as in

⌣ *ocean*. Write Exercise No. 21, page 120.

To become a proficient shorthand writer it is not only necessary to learn the principles of shorthand, but to train the hand to rapidly and accurately execute the characters. The student should, therefore, be watchful and not allow himself to neglect either portion of the work. Each lesson should be thoroughly studied, and frequent reviews should be made of all previous lessons. This will prepare the mind to act quickly. Single words, phrases, and sometimes whole sentences should be selected from the engraved pages and written hundreds of times. This will furnish the necessary training for the hand.

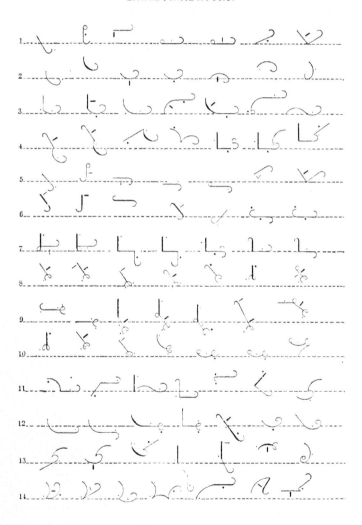

The Halving Principle.

/ 189. Any stroke consonant, except *w, y, ng*, and *mp*, may be made half its usual length to add the sound of *t* or *d*. The sound of *t* is usually added to light characters, and the sound of *d* to heavy characters. (See lines 1 and 2.) This rule, however, is only general, as either *t* or *d* may be added to either the light or the heavy strokes.

190. The half-length characters are vocalized the same as a character containing a final circle, loop, or hook ; that is, a vowel written before a half-length is read before the stroke, while one placed after is read between the stroke and the *t* or *d*. See line 6.

191. The position for half-lengths is as follows : — First position above the line ; second, on the line ; third, just below the line. See lines 6, 7 and 8.

192. Inasmuch as *w, y, ng*, and *mp* are never halved, a distinction may be made between *t* added to *r, l, m*, and *n* and *d* added to the same stroke, by shading the stroke in the latter case.

       rt,   lt,   mt,   nt,

       rd,   ld,   md,   nd,

See line 9.

193. When standing alone *lt* should be made upward, and *ld*, downward.

194. When *s* is halved it may be written upward if more convenient. See line 10.

195. Double or triple consonants may be made half-length and are then read just like the full lengths, the *t* or *d* expressed by halving invariably coming last. See lines 11 to 14.

Study, transcribe, write, correct, and rewrite as directed for previous lessons.

Write Exercise No. 22, page 121.

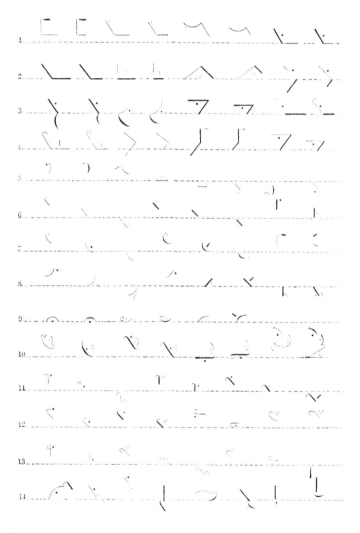

The Halving Principle — Continued.

196. Strokes to which the final hooks have been added may be made half-length; in which case the *t* or *d* is read after the hook.   See lines 1 to 5.

197. While the *t* or *d* expressed by halving is read after all hooks, it is read before all final circles and loops.   See line 6.

198. If the hook and circle are used together at the end of a half-length stroke, the *t* or *d* expressed by halving is read between the hook and circle.   See line 7.

199. The syllable *ted* is represented by half-length *t*, and the syllable *ded* by half-length *d*, as in line 8.

200. The half-length *t* or *d* should be disjoined after strokes with which it forms no angle.   See line 9.

201. *Upward* *r* and *h* should be made half-length only when joined to some other stroke or when some hook is attached; because simple half-length *upward* *r* might be mistaken for *cht*, and half-length *h* for *chft*.   See line 11.

202. The halving principle cannot be used in such words as are given in the 12th line, because the character preceding the final *t* or *d* does not form an angle with the character preceding it, and, therefore, it would be impossible to tell the exact point of juncture.

203. The stroke *t* or *d* must be used when the word ends with a vowel preceded by *t* or *d*, and when there are two vowels between *t* or *d* and the preceding stroke.   See lines 13 and 14.

204. Thus the proper use of the halving principle adds to the legibility of the notes in the same manner as does the proper use of the circles and loops.   Consult paragraph 157.

After studying and practicing this lesson, review the Halving Principle as a whole.   Write Exercise No. 23, page 121.

THE HALVING PRINCIPLE.

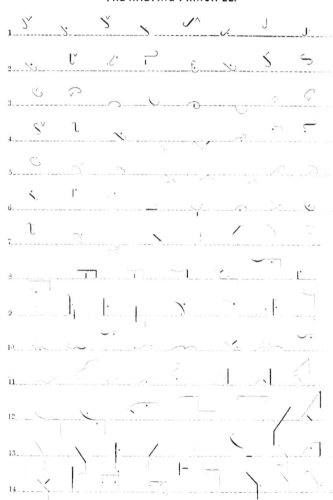

The Doubling Principle.

205. The doubling principle applies to curves only.

206. Doubling the length of *mp*, or *mb* adds *er*. See line 1.

207. Doubling the length of *ng* adds *ker* or *ger*. See line 2.

208. Doubling the length of *any other curve* adds *ther*, *ter*, or *der*. See line 3.

209. The point of commencing a double length for a given position should be the same as for a single length; that is, the first half of the double-length determines the position of the word. See lines 4 and 5.

210. Vowels placed after double-length curves must be read before the added syllable. When a word ends with a vowel sound the doubling principle cannot be used immediately before it. *Anger* should be written ⁀, but *angry* ⌣.

211. A final circle, loop, or hook may be attached to the double-lengths, such appendage being read last; as *northern.*

Special Vocalization.

212. It is sometimes desirable to intervocalize the double consonants; that is, write the vowel so as to have it read between the sound expressed by the stem and the sound of *l* or *r.*

213. When a dash vowel or a diphthong is to be read between the parts of a double consonant, strike the vowel through the stroke, or, if more convenient, place the first position vowel just at the beginning, or the third position vowel just at the end of the stroke. See lines 10 and 11.

214. To express dot vowels between the parts of a double consonant, write a small circle at the side of the stroke and in the position of the desired vowel. It is generally best to write the circle before the stroke if the vowel is long, and after it if the vowel is short. See lines 12 and 13. Write Exercise No. 24, page **122.**

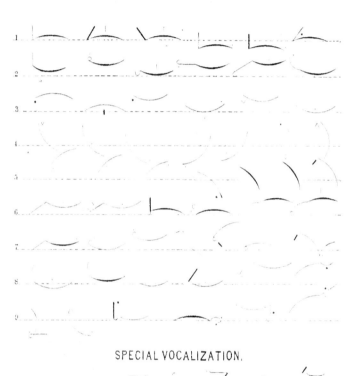

SPECIAL VOCALIZATION.

Word-Signs and Phrases.

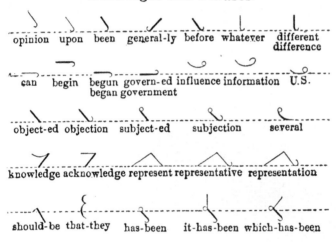

opinion   upon   been   general-ly   before   whatever   different
                                                     difference

can   begin   begun   govern-ed   influence   information   U.S.
                began   government

object-ed   objection   subject-ed   subjection   several

knowledge   acknowledge   represent   representative   representation

should-be   that-they   has-been   it-has-been   which-has-been

It will be found to be true economy to always use the
very best material not only in class-work but in practice.
Students sometimes fall into the habit of using poor pencils. This should be avoided. The stenographer cannot
produce good results with poor tools any more than can
the carpenter or mechanic of any kind. It is necessary
also, in order to work under the best conditions, that
paper of good quality and properly ruled be used. Fools-
cap is not good for shorthand purposes because the lines
are too close together. Neither should the inexperienced
stenographer write on unruled paper, or paper which he
may rule himself by hastily drawing lines across it. This
is almost sure to develop a large sprawling hand, which is
very undesirable.

Write Exercise No. 25, page 124.

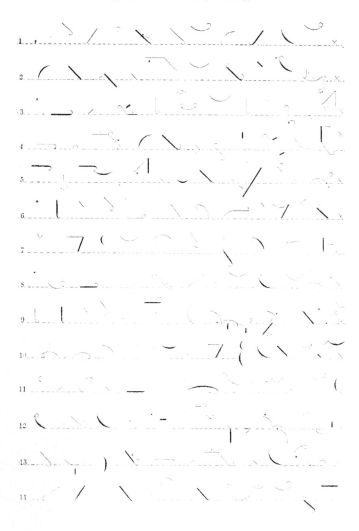

Half-Length Word-Signs.

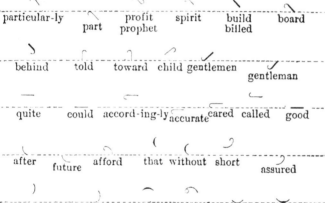

partieular-ly   part   profit prophet   spirit   build billed   board

behind   told   toward   child gentlemen   gentleman

quite   could   accord-ing-ly   accurate   eared   called   good

after   future   afford   that   without   short   assured

astonish-ed astonishment   establish-ed establishment   imme- diate-ly   somewhat   nature   under hundred

In writing half-lengths, word-signs or otherwise, be care
ful not to make the characters too large. It is better to
make such characters a little less than half the usual length
than to make them too long. The student will find that as
he writes more rapidly the tendency will be to make all the
characters larger than he did at the beginning, when his
writing was necessarily very slow. This tendency should
be overcome, as a very large hand is not usually capable of
so great speed in the end and does not look so well as a
small, neat hand. Also avoid leaving too much space between the words. There should not be more than one-
quarter of an inch between the characters and they may
be written as close as one-eighth of an inch with excellent results. Train the hand not only to move quickly
while executing the characters, but to move rapidly from
one character to another. It is only by giving attention to
all the little things that real proficiency will be attained.

Write Exercise No. 26, page 125.

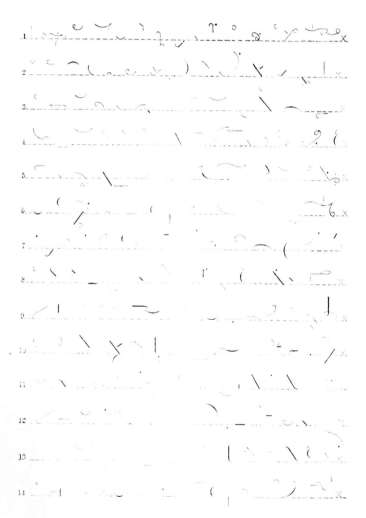

Prefixes.

215. *Con-* or *com-* is indicated by a dot placed immediately before the beginning of an outline.   See line 1.

216. *-Con-*, *-com-*, or *-cog-*, in the middle of a word, is expressed by disjoining that part of the outline which follows *con*, *com*, or *cog* from the part which precedes it.   Place the disjoined parts close to each other, the latter a little below as well as a little to the right of the former.   See line 2.

217. *Contra-*, *contri-*, *contro-*, or *counter-* is represented by a short oblique tick disjoined, as in line 3.   [See line 4.

218. *Circum-* or *self-* is represented by disjoined circle *s*.

219. *In-*, *en-*, or *un-* is expressed by a backward curl before any evolute circle, as in line 5.

220. *Magna-* or *magni-* is expressed by writing *m* over the beginning of the rest of the outline.   See line 6.

Affixes.

221. *-Ing*, as an affix, should generally be expressed by the stroke *ng*, but, when an inconvenient outline would result from the use of the stroke, a small dot may be used.   See line 7.

222. *-Ings* is expressed by a disjoined circle *s* placed near the end of an outline.   See line 7.

223. *-Ing the* is expressed by disjoining the tick *the* and writing it in place of the dot *ing*, as at the end of line 8.

224. *-Ble* or *-bly* is expressed by *b*.   See line 8.

225. *-Ful* or *-fore* is expressed by *f*.   See line 9.

226. *-Ever* is indicated by stroke *v*.   See line 10.

227. *-Ship* is represented by *sh*.   See line 11.

228. *-Self* is represented by circle *s* and *-selves* by *sez*. See line 12.

229. *-Ality*, *-ility*, or *-arity* at the end of words is indicated by disjoining the stroke which immediately precedes *-ality*, *-ility*, or *-arity* from the rest of the outline.   See line 13.   Write Exercise No. 27, page 126.

EXERCISE ON PREFIXES.

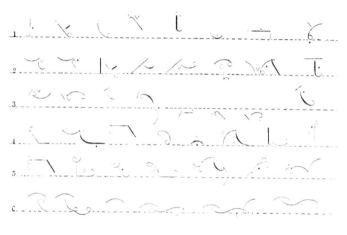

EXERCISE ON AFFIXES.

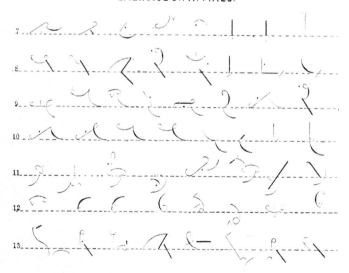

Word-Signs.

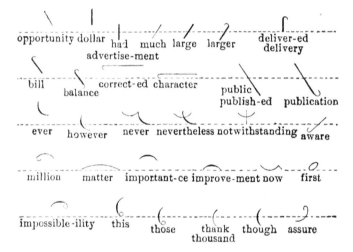

All the word-signs necessary for a speed of 140 or 150 words per minute on average matter have now been given, and the student is urged to make a careful and thorough review of the same. As already suggested, it is a good plan to always have a complete list of the word-signs at hand to study and practice at leisure moments. *They cannot be learned too well.* Students sometimes get the idea that the frequently occurring words are not very important, and that they can be distinguished by the context even if written incorrectly. This is a decided error. *Both speed in writing and accuracy in reading depend to a great extent upon a perfect knowledge of the word-signs.*

Write Exercise No. 28, page 127.

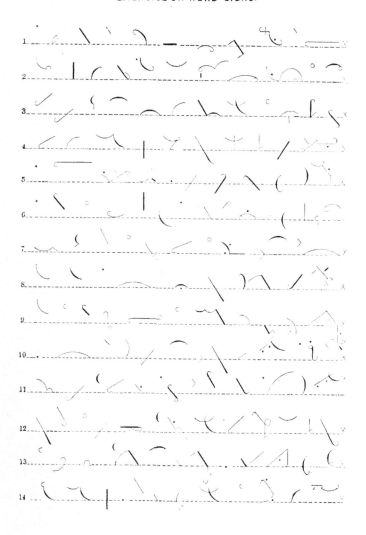

Review Exercises.

96. What is represented by a large initial hook on the *s* side of *t, d, k,* and *g* ?

97. Analyze *quick* and *queen.*

98. How may *s* be expressed before *twa, dwa, kwa* or *qwa* ?

99. What is represented by a large hook at the beginning of *m, n,* and *upward r* ? At the beginning of *l* ?

100. Why should the hook be made large in this series?

101. Are *ml, nl, rl,* and *lr* double consonants?

102. Are they ever used when there is an intervening vowel?

103. Describe the *shun* hook.

104. What is expressed by a large final hook on the opposite side from *shun* ?

105. To what characters is the *ther* hook added ?

106. How is circle *s* added to large final hooks?

107. How is *shun* added to circles?

108. To what extent may the *s-shun* curl be vocalized ?

109. What is expressed by the halving principle ?

110. What characters are never halved?

111. How are the half-lengths vocalized?

112. Give the rule for the position of the half-length characters.

113. What distinction may be made between *lt* and *ld, rt* and *rd, mt* and *md, nt* and *nd* ?

114. In what order are consonants, expressed by a half-length stroke with a final hook, to be read ?

115. In what order are consonants, expressed by a half-length stroke with a final circle or loop, to be read?

116. In what order are the consonants, expressed by a half-length stroke with a final circle on the *n* side, to be read?
117. When should half-length *t* or *d* be disjoined?
118. Under what conditions may *h* and *upward r* be halved?
119. Should a character be made half-length after another with which it forms no angle?
120. When must the stroke *t* or *d* be used?
121. To what characters does the doubling principle apply?
122. What is added to *mp* by doubling? To *ng?* To any other curve?
123. Explain the position of double-lengths
124. How are the double-lengths vocalized?
125. When final circles, loops, or hooks are attached to the double-lengths, how are they read?
126. What is the prefix for *con* or *com ?*
127. How may *con, com,* or *cog* be expressed in the middle of a word?
128. What is the prefix for *contra, contri, contro,* or *counter ?* For *circum* or *self ?*
129. What is expressed by a backward curl before an evolute circle?
130. What is the prefix for *magna* or *magni ?*
131. What is the affix for *ing ?* For *ings ?* For *ble* or *bly ?*
132. What is the affix for *ful* or *fore ?* For *ever ?* For *ship ?* For *self ?* For *selves ?*
133. How is *ility ality* or *arity* indicated at the end of words.

TABLE OF

	s-	-s	sez-	-sez	st-	-st	-str	w-	-l	s-l	-r	s-r	ss-r	-f	-fs
P															
B															
T															
D															
Ch															
J															
K															
G															
F															
V															
Th															
Th															
S															
Z															
Sh															
Zh															
L															
R															
R															
M															
N															
Ng															
W															
Y															
H															
Mp															

-n	-ns	-nsez	-nst	-nstr	-t	-ts	-ft	-fts	-nt	-nts	-w	-shun	-thr -tr -dr	-s shun	-ns shun

The Word-signs.

PHONOGRAPHICALLY ARRANGED.

opportunity	be	billed, build
up	object-ed	able-to
hope, happy	to-be	behind
appear	subject-ed	it
princip^{le}_{al-ly}	member	itself
practice	remember-ed	truth
opinion	number-ed	tell, till
upon	bill	until
happen	balance	whatever
particular-ly part	been	toward
spirit	before	told
profit, prophet	objection	dollar
by	subjection	do
	board	had

Where no dotted line appears, words are in second position.

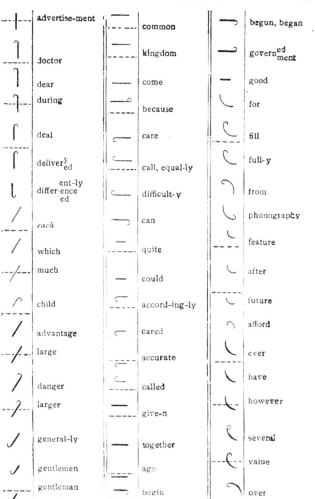

advertise-ment	begun, began
doctor	govern ed ment
dear	good
during	for
deal	fill
deliver y ed	full-y
ent-ly differ-ence ed	from
each	phonography
which	feature
much	after
child	future
advantage	afford
large	ever
danger	have
larger	however
general-ly	several
gentlemen	value
gentleman	over

common
kingdom
come
because
care
call, equal-ly
difficult-y
can
quite
could
accord-ing-ly
cared
accurate
called
give-n
together
ago
begin

	every, very
	valued
	think
	thank
	thousand
	three
	them
	though
	these
	this
	those
	either
	there, their
	other
	that
	without
	astonish
	establish

	was
	wish
	shall, shalt
	sure-ly
	assure
	short
	assured
	usual-ly
	pleasure
	will
	here
	are
	Lord
	are
	where
	aware
	him, am
	important-ce

	improved ment
	impossible-ity
	million
	Mr.
	remark able ably
	more
	somewhat
	immediate-ly
	matter
	in, any
	influence
	now
	U. S.
	when
	near, nor
	information
	under, hundred
	nature

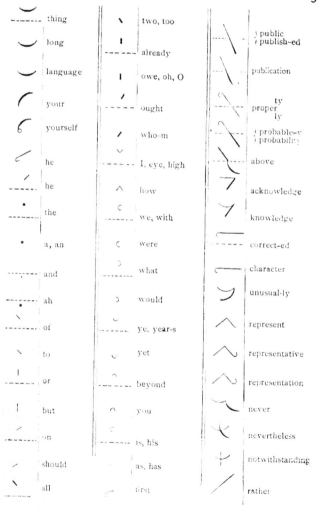

thing	two, too	public / publish-ed
long	already	publication
language	owe, oh, O	proper ty / ly
your	ought	probable-y / probability
yourself	who-m	above
he	I, eye, high	acknowledge
he	how	knowledge
the	we, with	correct-ed
a, an	were	character
and	what	unusual-ly
ah	would	represent
of	ye, year-s	representative
to	yet	representation
or	beyond	never
but	you	nevertheless
on	is, his	notwithstanding
should	as, has	rather
all	first	

Formation of Outlines.

230. Since many of the consonant sounds are represented in more than one way, it follows that a given word
may be written with several different outlines, each of
which will express the consonant sounds of the word ; for
instance, the consonant sounds in *store* are *s-t-r*, which
combination may be written in shorthand in at least eleven
different ways, as follows : —

231. To a successful stenographer, however, a consonant
outline is something more than the representation of the
consonant sounds of a word. It is the representation of
the consonant sounds of a word *in such a manner as to indicate to the greatest extent possible both* WHAT *and* WHERE
the vowel is. It is right here that many fail. They cannot read their notes because there is no clue to the vowel
element. To them, any one of the eleven outlines given
above conveys the same meaning as any other, when to
the well-trained stenographer each has its peculiar meaning.

232. We have said that the consonant outline of a word
should indicate *what* and *where* the vowel is. a. *The position of the outline indicates* WHAT *the vowel is.* b. *The manner of writing the consonants indicates* WHERE *the vowel is.*
Thus the vowel element, though invisible, is a very important factor in reading shorthand, and the extent to
which the student takes advantage of this, will determine,
to a great extent, the legibility of his notes.

233. It is already understood that writing an outline in
the first position indicates that the vowel (or if more than
one, the accented vowel) in that word is one of the six first-

place vowels; namely, ē, ạ, ĭ, ŏ, ĭ, oi. In the same manner, writing an outline in the second position indicates that the vowel is either ā, ō, ĕ, or ŭ, and in the third position that the vowel is either ä, ōō, ă, ŏŏ, ow or ū.

234. The criticism may be made that position only tells that the vowel is one of several. As a matter of fact, it tells so definitely, that the practiced writer only finds it necessary to insert an average of one vowel in about one hundred words. First, because most outlines, when in a certain position, represent but one word. Second, when a given outline in a certain position represents more than one word, as ⌐ for *tick* or *talk*, the context in a sentence will almost always lead to the proper word. In the comparatively few cases where this would not be sufficient, the vowel should be written.

235. It is also true, that, to a far greater extent than would at first appear, the manner of writing the consonants may be made to indicate *where* the vowel is. A very simple illustration of this is found in the words ⟍ *oar*, and ⟋ *row*. The full significance of the rules for upward and downward *r*, and *l* (paragraphs 59 and 60) will now be appreciated. These rules, as well as those for the use of circles *s* and *sez* ; loops *st* and *str* ; semicircles *w* and *y* ; hooks *l*, *r*, *n*, *f* or *v*, *w*, *shun*, and *ther* ; the halving principle; and the doubling principle, should now be thoroughly reviewed.

236. It will be found excellent practice to select words from any of the engraved pages, and mentally give the reason for each consonant being written as it is. To illustrate, we will take some of the outlines given at the end of paragraph 230, and placing each to a proper word, give the reasons for thus writing it.

237. ⟍ *store :* *st* loop to indicate that there is no vowel before the *s* nor between the *s* and the *t* ; *downward r* to indicate that *r* ends the word.

238. ⟋--- *story : st* loop to indicate that there is no vowel before *s* nor between the *s* and *t ; upward r* to indicate that there is a final vowel.

239. ⌐ *stray :* circle *s* to indicate that there is no vowel before the *s ;* double consonant *tr* to indicate that there is no vowel between the *t* and the *r*.

240. ⟍ *astray :* stroke *s* to indicate that there is a vowel before *s ;* double consonant *tr* to indicate that there is no vowel between the *t* and the *r*.

241. ⟍ *austere :* stroke *s* to indicate that there is a vowel before the *s ; t* expressed by the halving principle to indicate that there is but one vowel between the *t* and the *r ; down-ward r* to indicate that there is no vowel after the *r*.

242. ⟋--- *history : h* may be omitted in words of frequent occurrence; stroke *s* to indicate that there is a vowel be-fore the *s ; t* expressed by the halving principle to indicate that there is but one vowel between the *t* and the *r; up-ward r* to indicate that there is a vowel after the *r*.

243. ⟍, *estuary :* stroke *s* to indicate that there is a vowel before *s ;* stroke *t* to indicate that there are two vowels be-tween the *t* and the *r ; upward r* to indicate that there is a vowel after the *r*.

244. ⟍-- *satire :* circle *s* to indicate that there is no vowel before the *s ;* stroke *t* to indicate that there is a vowel be-tween the *s* and *t ;* stroke *r* to indicate that there is a vowel between the *t* and the *r ; r* made *downward* to indicate that *r* ends the word.

245. ᑒ *satirize:* circle *s* to indicate that there is no vowel before the *s;* stroke *t* to indicate that there is a vowel between the *s* and the *t;* stroke *r* to indicate that there is a vowel between the *t* and the *r; r* made *upward* to indicate that there is a vowel after the *r;* circle *s* to indicate that there is no vowel after the *s.*

246. ᑐ *oyster;* stroke *s* to indicate that there is a vowel before the *s; ter* expressed by the doubling principle to indicate that there is no vowel after *ter.*

247. If this idea were fully and universally carried out, we should hear much less of the stenographer who "cannot read his notes." In reality, no such person exists, for the person who cannot read his notes is not a stenographer.

248. One of the beauties of the present system of shorthand is that it is not necessary to learn and arbitrarily remember the outline for each word. On the other hand, it should be the aim of the beginner to so thoroughly master the principles that the correct outline for a word can be quickly formed by the application of these principles, even though the word may never have been seen or heard before.

249. Illustrations of the proper application of principles are, however, an aid to the student. These have already been given in abundance; but we present upon the three following engraved pages the outlines for many frequently occurring words, the same appearing also in ordinary type on the alternate printed pages. These pages should be studied in the following manner:

1. Read from the engraved page, referring to the printed page *only when necessary.*

2. Copy the engraved page, recalling the word expressed by each outline.

3. Give the reason for the use of each stroke, circle, hook, etc., in each word.

4. Write from the printed page and compare your notes with the engraved page, making necessary corrections.

5. Write each outline many times for the purpose of developing the ability to execute rapidly. For this purpose, one outline can be written hundreds of times, making it each time accurately, but gradually increasing in speed.

OUTLINES.

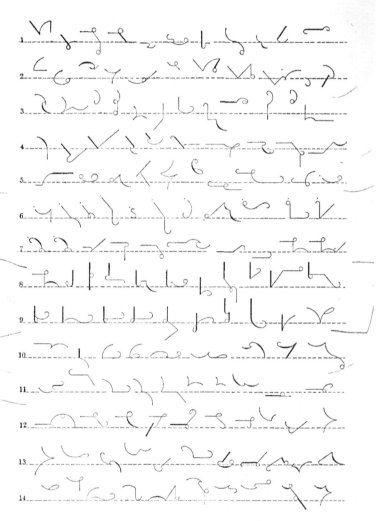

Key to Outlines on page 88.

1. Ability, absolute, acceptance, accessible, accountant, acquaintance, advocate, affairs, affidavit, agent, agreement.

2. Alike, allowance, ambition, annual, answer, anticipate, apologize, apparatus, apparently, around, arrange.

3. Arrival, ascertain, assign, assistance, assume, attach, attention, attractive, augments, authority, authorize, automatic.

4. Await, barrel, bearer, benefit, between, broker, cancel *or* counsel, canvass, capacity, carrying.

5. Catalogue, census, certify, cheaper, chenille, civilized, classical, classification, closely, commence.

6. Community, compare, compensation, competition, complaint, computation, concession, conservative, consignment, construction, contrary.

7. Conversant, conversation, country, county, coupons, criminal, current, cushion, custom, customary.

8. Customer, debtors, decide, decline, defective, defense, demand, depositor, derived, derricks, description.

9. Destination, dimension, discretion, discussion, dispatch, dissolution, dividends, division, duly, earliest.

10. Economy, editor, election, element, eminence, enclosed, endeavor, energy, enforce.

11. Engraved, equip, erection, error, escape, esteem, esteemed, evening, exact, excellent.

12. Excelsior, exception, excessive, exchange, exertions, explain, extent *or* extend, fault, federal, file.

13. Filter, fixed, flavor, fortunate, foundry, friction, generous, grocery, habits, hardly, heavy.

14. Honest, honesty, illumination, imitation, imperative, implicit, inclined, increase, indispensable, individual.

OUTLINES.

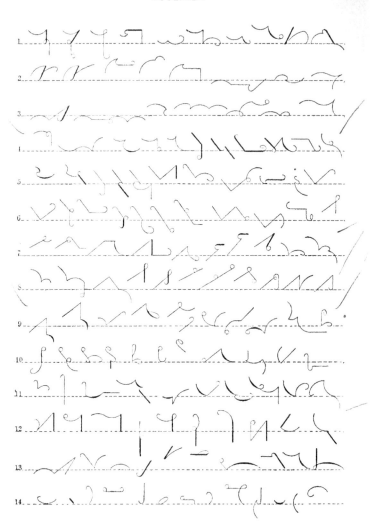

Key to Outlines on page 90.

1. Industry, injustice, institution, integrity, intention, intimation, invent, invoice, jealousy, laborer.

2. Legislation, legislator, likewise, limit, locality, mackerel, maintain, manual.

3. Margin, maximum, method, minimum, miscellaneous, moment, month.

4. Mystery, namely, nothing, notice, notify, obedience, objectionable, obligations, observation, occupation, officer.

5. Ordinary, ostensible, patent, payable, penalty, period, permission, perusal, photograph, plaintiff, porter.

6. Portion, positive, precaution, precedent *or* president, profession, propose, prospect, purpose, pursue, quotations, receipt.

7. Recent, reciprocate, rectify, reduction, refuse, regard, regret, rejoice, remain, reminder.

8. Remit, remittance, repair, reside, resident, resort, resource, response, restrain, retail, retain.

9. Retard, retired, return, revised, risen, roof, safely, salary, sample, scientific, settlement.

10. Situation, specify, specimen, splendid, statement, station, supply, survey, tendency, thorough, traffic.

11. Treatment, treaty, trunk, unavoidable, undoubtedly, various, veneration, vicinity, violation, welfare.

12. Yesterday, Sunday, Monday, Tuesday, Wednesday, Thursday, Friday, Saturday, January, February.

13. March, April, May, June, July, August, September, October, November, December.

14. One, two, three, six, ten, first, second, third, sixth, tenth, hundred, thousand, million.

Contracted Outlines.

250. Consonant sounds that are obscure, as *k* in *anxious*, need not be represented. Words containing several consonant sounds will generally be suggestive even if a somewhat prominent sound is omitted. See lines 1 to 3, page 93.

251. Words having but one consonant sound, but having two or more vowel sounds, should generally have one of the vowels written. See line 4, page 93.

252. A word-sign may be used as part of a longer word, joining to the word-sign whatever is necessary to complete the word. In such case, the word-sign must retain its position. If two word-signs are thus united, the first is generally put in position. See lines 5 to 7, page 93.

253. While many outlines — especially long ones — will be sufficiently suggestive without the aid of position, there are some words that are distinguished *only by position*. See line 8, page 93.

254. Such positive and negative words as are given in the 9th and 10th lines should be carefully distinguished.

255. Words containing the same consonant sounds but of different or opposite meanings should be distinguished by a systematic difference in the outline, if possible. See line 11, page 93. If this is not possible, a vowel may be inserted (line 12) or an arbitrary difference of outline may be made. See line 13, page 93.

256. It is sometimes desirable in writing derivatives to keep the outline for the primitive in the position it would occupy if alone, and to it add whatever is necessary to complete the word.   ﹏ *need*, ⌐ *needless;* ﹏ *end*, ⌐ *endless.*

257. Two or more prominent consonants in a word of frequent occurrence may sometimes be used as a contraction for that word. See line 14, page 93.

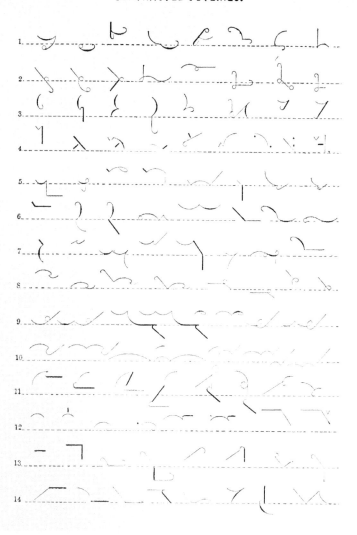

Key to Contracted Outlines on page 93.

1. Anxious, sanction, distinction, function, suggestion, frequent, eloquent, tempt.

2. Postpone, postoffice, postage, testimony, mistake, transaction, transpose, transact.

3. Within, withdraw, withhold, hesitation, assignment, trustworthy, intelligent, intelligence.

4. Idea, obey, Iowa, arrow, Ohio, oil, era, payee, iota.

5. Undertake, understand, almost, almighty, to-morrow, to-day, forward, afterward.

6. Altogether, therefore, thereby, somehow, anything, become, everything, something.

7. Although, onward, underneath, anywhere, anybody, natural, misunderstood, overcome.

8. Imminent, eminent, prominent, permanent, except, accept, position, possession.

9. Necessary, unnecessary, navigable, unnavigable, modest, immodest, necessarily, unnecessarily.

10. Moral, immoral, material, immaterial, moderate, immoderate, mature, immature.

11. Legal, illegal, logical, illogical, resistible, irresistible, resolute, irresolute.

12. Meet, omit, motion, emotion, migrate, immigrate, keep *or* copy, occupy.

13. God, guide, protection, production, writer, reader, support, separate.

14. Regular-ity, irregular-ity, peculiar-ity, capable, familiar, New York, develop, perform.

Phrasing.

258. Phrasing is the act of writing two or more words with a single outline.

259. While there is a diversity of opinion among stenographers regarding the extent to which phrasing should be employed, there is no doubt that, within certain limits, it is very desirable. It is desirable because it facilitates writing without retarding the reading; indeed, notes properly phrased are more legible than when each word is written separately.

260. In forming phrases the following rules should be observed: —

1. Phrase only such words as have a grammatical connection.

2. Phrase only when the outlines can be easily united in writing.

3. Do not form phrases of inconvenient length, or that extend too far above or below the line of writing.

261. There are two distinct methods of phrasing. The first and simpler is to unite the regular outlines of the words composing the phrase; as *you-will-be-likely*. The second method is to consider the phrase as a single word and by the use of the various principles express its consonant sounds in the easiest way; as _____ *in-re-gard*.

262. When the regular outlines are joined, the first word of a phrase is usually put in position and the following words must accommodate themselves to the position of the first. See lines 1–6, page 96. It is, however, that word which, out of position, would be illegible, which must be given its position. See line 7, page 96.

263. When *must* is other than the last word of a phrase it may be written with *m* and circle *s* instead of *m* and *st* loop. See line 8, page 96.

264. The ticks *the*, *a*, *an*, and *and* are not considered as having positions of their own, but always accommodate themselves to the position of the word or words with which they are joined. See line 9, page 96.

265. When a word which ends with a circle is followed by one which begins with a circle, the two circles may be united into one large circle. See line 10, page 96.

266. Phrases of great value in certain lines of work may be formed by intersecting prominent characters in the phrase. Stroke *s* thus intersected may be used to represent *society*; *sh*, *association*; *k*, *company*; *d*, *department*; *t*, *committee*; *j*, *agent*. See lines 12 to 14, page 96.

PHRASES.

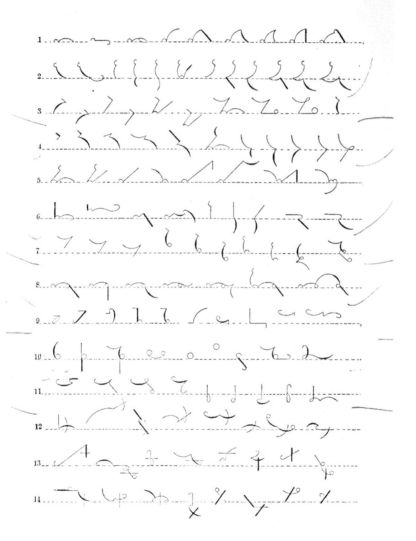

Key to Phrases on page 96.

1. You may, you can, you must, you will, you will be, you will have, you will think, you will do, you will remember.

2. We have, we have known, we think, we think that, we think so, we think you will, we shall, we shall be, we shall have, we shall not be, we shall not have, we shall never.

3. Of your, to your, of which, to which, of which you are, to which you are, in which you may, in which case, in such cases, of them.

4. All the, all the way, on the way, in the way, by the way, that which you may, for that, for them, for your, for which, for such.

5. With which you may, with which you are, you are, are you, you are right, you are wrong, are you ready, are you sure.

6. Do you mean, did you mention, you should be, you should endeavor, with it, it was, which was, can be, can have.

7. In each, in which, in much, of these, of this, of those, we think you, we thank you, those who are, in this place.

8. You must be, you must do, you must have, you must not, you must not think, we think you must be, you must always be.

9. A first, a general, and there, and do you, and this, and will, send a, take a, when a, when a man.

10. This is, it is said, in this city, as soon as, as has, is his, as has been, in this section, there is something.

11. In regard, in reply, in response, in relation, at first, at once, at any rate, at last, at sometime.

12. Temperance Society, Literary Society, Bible Society, Missionary Society, Singing Society, Improvement Association, Savings Association, Medical Association.

13. Railroad Co., American Express Co., Trust Co., Investment Co., Oil Co., Shorthand Department, War Department, Postoffice Department.

14. Executive Committee, Finance Committee, Ways and Means Committee, Traveling Agent, Special Agent, Book Agent, Insurance Agent, Freight Agent.

Phrasing — Continued.

267. When *I* is the first word of a phrase it may be written with either the first or last stroke of the usual character. The first stroke must always be written downward and the last upward. Select that stroke which forms the better angle with the following word. See lines 1–5.

268. *We* or *with* may be expressed by the initial *w* hook. See lines 6 and 7, page 99.

269. *You*, in phrasing, may be inverted in order to secure good joinings. See line 8, page 99.

270. *There*, *their*, *other*, or *they-are* may be expressed by doubling a preceding curve. See lines 9 and 10, page 99.

271. *There* or *their* may be expressed by adding the *ther* hook to a preceding straight stroke. See line 11, page 99.

272. *Own* or *than* may be expressed by adding the *n* hook to a preceding word. See line 12, page 99.

273. *All* or *will* may be expressed by adding the *l* hook to a preceding word. See line 13, page 99.

274. *Are* may be expressed by adding the *r* hook to a preceding word. See line 14, page 99.

Key to Phrases on page 99.

1. I am, I am glad, I am very, I am very glad, I am sure, I am very sure, I am sorry, I am inclined.

2. I have, I have known, I have seen, I have said, I have done, I think, I think so, I think you will, I think you may, I find.

3. I fear, I fear you will be, I shall, I shall be, I shall have, I shall never, I wish, I wish to, I wish to be, I wish you.

4. I will, I will have, I will think, I will do, I can, I cannot, I can be, I can never.

5. I do, I had, I had been, I had many, I mean, I must, I must be sure, I need not, I never.

6. We will, we will think, we will be, we will try, we are, we are aware, we are inclined, we are sorry, we are certain.

7. We may *or* with him, we may mention, we must, we must also, we must always, we must be, with me *or* with my, we mean.

8. Should you, should you know, send you, when you can, forward you, I send you, I need you, I inclose you.

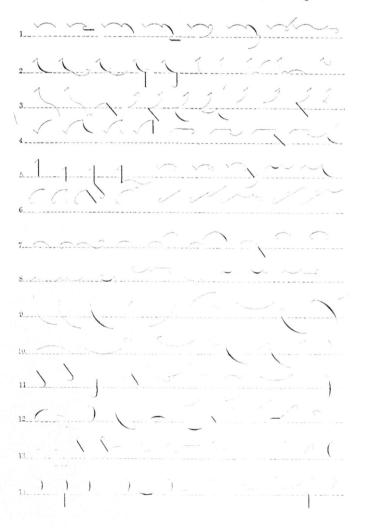

Key to Phrases on page 99.

9. If there *or* if their *or* if they are, for there *or* for their *or* for they are, have there *or* have their, think there *or* think their *or* think they are, wish there *or* wish their, will there *or* will their, are there *or* are their, in there *or* in their, value their, over there *or* over their.

10. Some other, no other, *or* know their, from there *or* from their, when there *or* when their, whenever there *or* whenever their, wherever there *or* wherever their, I think there *or* I think their *or* I think they are, so there *or* so they are.

11. Be there, by their, had there *or* had their, you will be there, finish their, furnish their, I am sure there is, in their places, was there *or* was their.

12. Your own, our own, their own, have their own, more than, sooner than, better than, rather than, greater than, further than.

13. At all, at all events, by all, by all means, in all, in all cases, in all such cases, for all, it will, which will, they will.

14. They are, they are said, they are certain, they are among, they are sometimes, which are, which are likely, which are necessary, which are dear, such are.

Phrasing — Continued.

275. *Not* may be expressed by the *n* hook and the halving principle. See line 1, page 101.

276. *It* may be expressed, after word-signs or outlines that end with a final straight stroke, by halving that stroke. See line 1, page 101.

277. *Us* may be expressed by circle *s* joined to a preceding word. See line 2, page 101.

278. *In* may be expressed by the backward *n* curl. Line 3.

279. *Have* or *of* may be expressed by adding the *v* hook to a preceding straight consonant. See line 4, page 101.

280. *He* may be expressed in phrasing by the tick *h*. See line 5, page 101.

281. *May-be* may be expressed by thickened *m*. See line 6.

282. *Con* or *com* may be expressed in a phrase, as in a word, by disjoining. See line 7, page 101.

283. *Of-the* may be expressed by proximity. See line 8.

284. *From-to* may be expressed by proximity. See line 9.

285. *A, and, the, of, to, or,* may sometimes be omitted in phrasing. See lines 10 and 11.

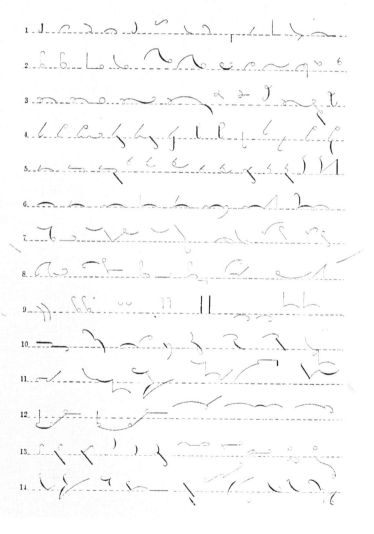

Key to Phrases on page 101.

1. Do not, will not, are not, may not, was not, we are not, for it, from it, at it, which it, take it, fetch it, make it.

2. Tell us, tells us, take us, for us, leave us, loves us, send us, let us, let us know, let us try, of us, with us.

3. In some, in some cases, in some things, in some other way, in spirit, in secret, in season, in as many as possible, in consideration.

4. Which have, such have, such have not known, which have been, which have not been, which have done, said to have, is said to have, out of, each of, much of, such of, such of them.

5. He may, he can, he can be, he is, he is not, he is in, he has, he has not, he has been, he would, he would be, he was, he was ready.

6. May be, he may be, you may be, it may be, which may be, you may be sure, you may be right, there may be some.

7. In this connection, in comparison, in competition, must confess, I will comply, I will not complain.

8. Wealth of the nation, remarks of the speaker, statement of the case, settlement of the account, laws of the country, center of the earth.

9. From hour to hour, from place to place, from year to year, from street to street, from day to day, from man to man, from time to time.

10. Again and again, over and over, more or less, two or three, east and west, mean to have, mean to be, for the first time.

11. Secretary of War, for a long time, in reply to your letter, in time of war, letter of credit, bill of lading.

12. At owner's risk, at sender's risk, my dear sir, my dear madam, my dear friend.

13. It will not, it will not be, which will not be, is it, h-as it, as it has been, my text, of course, first-class, as fast as, as far as.

14. We have received your letter, in order that, able to make, to be able to, we are in receipt of your letter, at hand, have been, I have been, very truly yours.

Conclusion.

All the principles of shorthand have been introduced and yet the student is, by no means, an accomplished stenographer. But, if they have been thoroughly learned, the foundation has been laid for the utmost skill as a shorthand reporter. Too much emphasis cannot be put upon the importance of knowing the principles perfectly. Young stenographers are apt, in their desire to gain speed, to endeavor to write *fast* before they are able to write *well*. This is not only dangerous because it is likely to develop illegibility, but it is not the shortest road to rapidity. As "speed is the result of familiarity with shorthand," the person who desires to become a rapid writer and a ready reader will not lay aside the manual when the principles have been gone over once or twice, but will review it again and again until it is thoroughly digested and assimilated.

When the student has secured this familiarity with the system of writing, and has practiced faithfully all the outlines, phrases, and exercises given in this book, he should have some one dictate to him as much as possible. The dictation should be easy at first and should never be given faster than it can be taken with absolute accuracy. Gradually the speed may be increased and more difficult matter selected until the writer is able to report verbatim anything that may be uttered. This is not to be accomplished except as *the result of much hard work*. While a few months of *hard work* will qualify one to accept a position as an amanuensis, yet no ambitious, energetic person will be willing to stop here. I would especially urge upon those who do accept positions where a speed of 100 or 125 words per minute is all that is required, that they continue regular, systematic study and practice, and thus obtain a reserve force, a surplus power. It may be needed at any time. As Garfield said, " If you are not too large for the place you occupy, you are too small for it."

Writing Exercises.

[To be written in connection with each lesson as directed.]

EXERCISE I.

CONSONANT OUTLINES.

Par. 12 *to* 33.

Write the consonant outlines of the following words:

Time, dime, check, catch, peck, keep, beak, cab, meek, deep, came, sheep, shave, beam, cheap, peach, fame, name, main, bail, pail, knave, knife, mail, balm, palm, calm, pity, match, pulley, book, funny, money, knock, heavy, lady, five, king, among, move, pony, hatch, mummy, honey, hung, lily, damage, engage, cash, coach, namely, nothing, deputy, apology, badge, know, yellow.

(In the following outlines use *upward r*). Rich, rage, rag, rock, review, rub, ripe, rash, right, wright, notary, wreck, zero, sherry, rosy, notoriety, purity, verify, park, tarry, marry, interior, inferior, terror, bearer.

EXERCISE II.

WORDS CONTAINING FIRST-POSITION VOWELS.

Par. 34 *to* 44.

Each, eat, me, my, if, in, boy, joy, time, dim, dime, talk, pea, bee, see, saw, ship, nip, nib, thy, chalk, mill, mile, pill, pile, boil, ice, ivy, meek, knock, niche, nigh, type, fog, top, knife, deny, filly, folly, pity, body, inch, oil, toil, cheek, dyke, noisy, oily, key, lee, eel, keel, tall, tile, doll, dock, lock, heath, she, gnaw, leave, beam, daub, pshaw, icy, eyes, pike, timely, ninny, lime, meek, teeth, peak, teach, balk, deal, jaw, tea, fee, thaw, thee, law, awl, talk, paw, chick, fib, chop, ditch, ill, tithe, ease, eke, leech, beak, beach, toy, pipe, jolly, bonny, poppy, cheap.

EXERCISE III.
WORDS CONTAINING SECOND-POSITION VOWELS.

Par. 45 *to* 49.

Ate, make, owed, know, up, duck, puffy, peck, bell, funny, fame, jug, neck, thumb, ape, fay, show, hate, head, leg, beck, maim, foam, loam, fellow, meadow, mull, pug, lug, ache, cake, Cato, money, honey, penny, mush, shame, both, poach, lucky, mellow, bub, jug, yea, knave, age, go, jay, oath, ace, bake, loathe, lame, poke, gnome, dumb, numb, chum, cape, nape, mope, halo, dummy, egg, faith, shave, dame, poke, name, deck, edge, oath, oak, decay, know, delay, vacate, also, shake, tongue, buggy, fetch, death, both.

EXERCISE IV.
WORDS CONTAINING THIRD-POSITION VOWELS.

Par. 50 *to* 54.

Ooze, ha, calm, balm, move, moody, downy, hatch, nap, hat, couch, boom, hash, duty, cube, endue, mouth, sham, push, book, coo, pussy, catch, add, pouch, vowel, undo, bouquet, lounge, tooth, pulley, cook, Fannie, gouge, towel, bough, vow, pew, few, cow, cuckoo, shook, map, nook, look, shaggy, rag, rap, bush, Hannah, mutiny, tank, family, palliate, out, cab, ensue, lack, lag, couch, shabby, cubic, mule, booth, use, ashy, duty, dupe, bank, downy, canny, chew, sue.

REVIEW EXERCISE No. 1.

SIMPLE WORDS, CONTAINING FIRST, SECOND AND **THIRD** PO-
SITION VOWELS.   PAGES 1-20.

Write the words in shorthand, being careful to place them in
proper position: Each, eat, ate, make, ooze, time, dime, check,
me, ode, calm, balm, know, my, hatch, peck, keep, beak, cab,
meek, if, in, up, palm, move, boy, moody, duck, downy, puffy,
joy, dim, talk, bell, nap, deep, came, sheep, shave, beam, cheap,
teach, fame, name, see, saw, funny, jug, hat, couch, boom, ship,
nip, neck, thumb, duty, cube, thy, mill, show, mouth, sham,
hate, head, mile, tile, leg, push, book, boil, ice, ivy, comb,
pussy, meek, catch, loam, knock, add, meadow, niche, nigh,
pouch, pug, undo, type, fog, knave, knife, mail, pity, lady,
heavy, money, pulley, match, five, king, among, pony, mummy,
honey, nothing, namely, coach, cash, engage, damage, lily,
hung, badge, top, deny, body, tooth, lounge, cook, ache, cake,
shame, gouge, inch, oil, toil, both, bathe, faith, bough, vow,
cheek, dike, pew, few, key, eel, shook, map, nook, zeal, zodiac,
Zion, lucky, like, mellow, lock, heath, jug, gnaw, she, yea, go,
beam, pshaw, shaggy, tank, dumb, loathe, oath, numb, chum,
eyes, timely, booth, awl, law, thaw, out, couch, shabby, fib,
chop, edge, tithe, cubic, decay, fetch, vouch, tongue, use, chew,
death, apology, effect, fact, monopoly, indemnity, unanimity,
indemnify, package, baggage, cabbage, luggage, tobacco,
Dakota, Toledo, Topeka, Chicago, Alabama, Kennebec,
Albany.

EXERCISE V.

Upward and Downward *r* and *l.*

Par. 56 to 61.

Rake, rogue, rob, row, rock, rim, ark, tire, fire, fiery, review, rhyme, pour, purr, poor, four, farm, form, rear, rack, arch, ear, army, room, earth, sherry, interior, inferior, arena, carry, jury, hour, hero, roar, fair, morrow, merino, dairy, orb, aright, urge, tear, tarry, lime, boil, foil, foul, fuel, coil, vile, vowel, dale, dell, jolly, jelly, bellow, loaf, love, lady, allow, guile, alive, lion, rally, rail, relay, roil, roily, fell, follow, hourly, mail, valley, alarm, lower, liar, fowl, pail, leaf, rely, toiler, loyalty, shower, arch, folly, rear, arrear, early, door.

EXERCISE VI.

Words Containing *s, z* and *sez.*

Par. 62 to 73.

Sit, sat, some, save, sing, stay, piece, does, goes, joys, race, guess, ties, chase, snows, signs, sour, seems, yes, ways, scheme, less, soaks, slope, smoke, sick, sledge, heroes, debase, advice, reasons, basin, beseech, dozen, hues, skip, muscles, dusty, incites, absolve, dissolve, locks, gossip, tools, dispatch, box, stacks, despoil, fastens, cellars, passive, ashes, dusk, besom, passes, pieces, bosses, boxes, abscess, abscesses, kisses, hisses, phases, successes, excesses, dispossesses, necessary, surfaces, chastises, noises, receipt, slope, surveys, notice, baser, spike, sly, tease, daze, toss, sail, sale, slay, recess, rose, roses, pass, loose, moss, knows, expose, phase, face, faces, phases.

EXERCISE VII.

WORDS CONTAINING *st*, *zd* AND *str*.

Par. 74 to 82.

Past, pastor, passed, pastors, baste, boasts, toasts, toast, toaster, toasters, beast, cast, casts, castor, castors, jest, jester, jests, jesters, guessed, mist, mister, muster, nest, haste, hissed, fosters, taste, gust, luster, gazed, vaster, rust, roasts, guest, tastes, duster, dusters, system, stole, faster, refused, best, just, justify, steal, store, tests, testify, star, storm, styles, invest, invests, destiny, artist, artists, utmost, surmised, deepest, register, rejoiced, stillest, fairest, digest, debased, revised, nests, mast, master, musters, atheist, atheistic, tease, dazed, amazed, forced, forest, forests, luster, still, stale, steamer, arrest, taskmaster, bolster, earnest, disposed, utmost, surmised, Rochester.

EXERCISE VIII.

WHEN TO USE CIRCLES AND LOOPS.

Par. 83 to 86.

Use, us, ask, moss, mossy, fuss, fussy, rose, rosy, same, maze, mazy, loose, lasso, case, sake, sauce, saucy, asp, pass, chaos, bias, zeal, sail, assail, espy, easy, isthmus, asthma, science, pious, gauzy, bestow, gusset, posy, essay, zinc, easel, sciatica, spy, espy, scion, scope, escape, oozing, zero, best, ecstasy, deposed, deposit, exposed, busy, resist, agency, jealous, jealousy, ensue, noise, noisy, resume, emphasis, emphasize, emphasized, sighs, eyes, dies, dizzy, days, daisy, decide, reside, escape, ease, easy, sleep, asleep.

REVIEW EXERCISE NO. 2.

WORDS CONTAINING UPWARD AND DOWNWARD *r* AND *l*, CIRCLES AND LOOPS. PAGES 21-31.

Write in shorthand without referring to the previous lessons: Past, sit, rake, rogue, view, rhyme, sat, race, guess, pastor, maze, arch, ear, ways, scheme, jester, jests, chaos, bias, carry, jury, debase, haste, science, pious, orb, aright, skip, muscles, roasts, guest, easel, sciatica, vile, vowel, sip, tools, best, ecstasy, refused, storm, styles, agency, jealous, allow, guile, passive, ashes, abscess, emphasis, utmost, emphasized, surmised, digest, excesses, dispossesses, follow, hourly, rely, toiler, receipt, slope, days, daisy, toss, moss, nose, door, luster, still, earnest, disposed, rob, pour, army, room, earth, hour, hero, urge, tear, dale, alive, nail, valley, loyalty, shower, some, save, ties, chase, lest, advice, reasons, dusty, incites, dispatch, box, dust, necessary, surveys, notice, sale, recess, expose, phase, taste, duster, just, justify, invests, deepest, register, lose, zeal, sail, assail, bestow, espy, spy, deposit, jealousy, decide, reside, escape, passage, rim, ark, tire, farm, morrow, lime, boil, foil, jolly, jelly, bellow, alarm, lower, relay, piece, does, signs, sour, smoke, beseech, absolve, passes, pieces, surface, rose, rosy, casks, mist, gazed, system, steel, store, tests, destiny, rejoiced, amazed, forced, arrest, saucy, essay, escape, exposed, busy, noise, noisy, asleep, zero, bolster, successes, gossip, yes, early, arrear, arena, review, aurora, zinc, rust, rusty, russet, roses, chastises, baser, dissolve, dairy, rally. Cincinnati, Mississippi, Syracuse, Jackson, Johnson, Smith, Mason, Paris, Minnesota.

EXERCISE IX.

Words Containing *w* and *y*.

Par. 87 *to* 100.

Weep, wet, watch, weave, wash, wig, weak, wave, **walk,**
web, wink, won, well, wag, yam, yoke, young, yawn, **wine,**
windy, wheel, whale, where, warm, weal, while, wan, ween,
Wednesday, window, Wheeling, once, whence, Yankee,
swore, swell, wail, swale, wealthy, welfare, warehouse,
sweep, wedge, wane, swap, swab, worm, work, wear,
swarthy, whereat, worst, wing, whim, woke, awoke, away,
await, witness, weed, sweet, Swede, watch, wade, wed,
young, wealth, welcome, wane, win, wool, worthy, **worth,**
wolf, weary, wall, swear, swan, swine, wit, **swim.**

EXERCISE X.

Heavy *m* and Tick *h*.

Par. 101 to 107.

Lamp, camp, dump, lump, pump, jump, pomp, stamp,
stump, champ, imp, romp, mumps, swamp, ambush, bamboo, ambitious, stumble, impeach, impedes, scamp, empire,
ambiguity, sympathy, home, hack, ham, her, why, hub,
heap, hammock, hassock, harrow, harm, whoa, hearth, hid,
hark, hop, height, hoar, hollow, whole, whistle, whig, hug,
havoc, hardy, whack, whisky, hoarse, hackney, hasten,
horizon, holiday, hair, homely, holier, haughty, helm, hem,
homely, holy, heal, whistler, Nahum, unholy, unhook, un-
wholesome, embalm, embank, embargo, embark, embassy,
embellish, embezzle, embody, hemp, hump.

EXERCISE XI.

WORD-SIGNS AND PHRASES.

Par. 108 *to* 119.

Be, it, do, which, come, give, for, think, will, are, your, he, that, we, I, how, you, is, as, of, to, on, should, the, a, and, of-the, to-the, to-you, you-should, you-may, if-you, you-will, of-it, of-your, it-will-be, you-will-be, you-will-think, you-may-go.

You-should study your lessons well. Do-you think he will go? Mary will come home for-the holidays. Will you give that book to Harry, and that pencil to Nellie? Which is your desk? You-may lay the book on the box in-the window. It is as I said; he has no right to leave the work for me. Take the best of-your fur and make a muff for-the lady.

EXERCISE XII.

WORD-SIGNS AND PHRASES

Par. 120 *to* 122.

Of, to, or, but, on, should, all, two, too, already, owe, oh, ought, who, whom, have, them, was, wish, shall, advantage, common, come, give, given, together, it-is, to-be, to-do, of-which, you-are, do-you, wish-to, we-are, we-will.

We-are happy to show you our stock of shoes. Pay your money and take your choice. Two of us will stay at home; all-the rest ought to go to Albany. Come to-the city and we-will see that you have-the advantages you wish. He was at home last week. The ring was given to him, and also the watch. We wish to read the manual together. We have but to say so and he will go or stay.

They have no reason to say that he is common. Who are you that you should be so haughty? You have given to me money that you owe to some one else.   We-will walk two miles as you already have. You too shall have-the advantages that they have.   He devises many schemes and boasts of his success. Are you disposed to give us the necessary tools for-the work which you wish us to-do? They will visit the museum together.

EXERCISE XIII.

WORD-SIGNS AND PHRASES.

Par. 123 *and* 124.

We, with, were, what, would, ye, year, yet, beyond, **you,** any, when, thing, long, him, usual, usually, we-were, what-would, would-you, is-the, you-are, are-you, have-you, for-the, in-which, be-willing, as-well-as, for-them.

We-were with you last year, yet you-will give us no **help.** What-would they do if we-were to leave them? Take-the next seat beyond you. Would they be-willing to leave the store for-a week or two? When he goes home take his books and lock them up in your room. Mary and her cousin will visit the fair together. All is as-well-as we wish. The ink was given you; the book you must pay for. He weighed well what he said; he will satisfy you.   Next year we hope to go west; what-would you give to go with us? He was anxious to live at home — that being best for his health. They were all too willing to receive money, and all too unwilling to pay it.   Two and two are four, and two less two is zero. They ought to-do well; they have had many advantages. His talk was harsh and rude. It-is warm by the register. Will you take a sail in my yacht?

REVIEW EXERCISE NO. 3.

ω HOOK AND SEMICIRCLE, THE y SEMICIRCLE, HEAVY m, TICK
h, WORD-SIGNS. PAGES 32-41.

Write in shorthand without referring to the previous lessons: Wet, weave, weak, lamp, camp, dump, swim, wall, weary, walk, wave, stamp, jump, hemp, embody, embezzle, web, wine, wink, well, young, yoke, yam, wealth, worth, worthy, wholesome, embalm, embank, embark, welcome, wool, ambush, bamboo, windy, where, while, wade, watch, sweet, weed, witness, weight, await, ambitious, stumble, impeach, whistler, homely, Wednesday, window, once, yankee, ambiguity, sympathy, home, hack, ham, her, why, holiday, haughty, swell, welfare, warehouse, hammock, hassock, harm, sweep, wedge, wane, work, wear, hark, height, hollow, whole, worst, whim, woke, awoke, away, Watson, Wilson, Winnipeg, Harrison, of, ought, common, be, will, is, and, you, think, for, how, a, the, I, given, we, should, on, that, come, which, he, to, your, do, it, are, as, his, has, have, them, or, was, wish, but, advantage, shall, all, already, together, whom, too, we-will, we-are, of-the, if-you, you-will, to-the, to-you, of-it, you-should, of-your, you-may, wish-to, do-you, you-are, of-which, to-do, to-be, it-is, owe, how, it-will-be. Honesty is the best policy. The love of money has caused the ruin of many. If you wish to succeed in your study you must be in earnest in your work. If you visit Chicago you should stop at Toledo. Write to your cousin and ask if she will come here this week for the purpose of which we spoke on Monday. If the boy comes the young lady will give him the key. It will be an advantage to you to be here in time to recite your lesson. Do you wish to speak to her?

EXERCISE XIV.

STRAIGHT DOUBLE CONSONANTS.

Par. 125 *to* 132.

Play, ply, pray, prow, plow, tray, grew, grow, gray, glow, clay, clue, drew, glue, cloy, acre, upper, utter, keeper, pauper, broom, brake, trice, drip, drop, trip, climb, cries, praise, blame, creep, clap, gleam, eagle, brook, couple, tidal, bridle, double, grapple, tiger, single, grew, glue, plump, crape, glass, crimp, crawl, clock, brake, bloom, group, try, blow, eager, able, paddle, block, cloy, prig, peer, bulk, opal, dire, places, grudge, pleas, dressed, tear, cloth, bear, bray, beagle, inveigle, creak, bleak, brackish, black, gall, gloss, bowls, bluster, climb, purple, pulp, plea, plum, press, breeze, cress, grace, gross, pressed, dressed, praised, crouch, crab, plume, pluck, plague, blubber, lubber, labor, grazed, plaster, blister, truck, drink, claw, brow, probe, title, bible, chill, tackle, pickle, truce.

EXERCISE XV.

CURVED DOUBLE CONSONANTS.

Par. 133 *to* 141.

Flee, free, fray, frame, fly, flow, fry, freak, flog, muffle, ruffle, raffle, manner, tanner, thrum, throb, thrash, flue, offer, travel, bevel, level, measure, treasure, throng, revel, shuffle, baffle, Ethel, Bethel, laver, special, especial, novel, hovel, shovel, tenor, banner, miner, plumber, drummer, flap, flabby, friar, froze, cavil, fissure, official, leisure, lasher, youthful, shrill, initial, throng, tinner, thinner, azure, throve, thresher, rumor, fleecy, Friday, shaver, flail, frail, fresh, flavor, flesh, thrumming, thrall, frugal, froth, frosty, fry, fluid, flung, flowery, shriek, shrimp, shrug, shrub, shrink, flag, flake, flame, flask, flax, floor, fluffy, flung, flurry, freckle, froth, awful, offer, evil, oval, ether, author, either, freshly, official, bushel.

EXERCISE XVI.

Triple Consonants. Par. 142 to 151.

Strip, strap, strike, straw, strew. stray, splay, display, stroke, struck, idle, saddle, settle, subtle, scrape, scribe, displease, describe, disagree, sister, stream, pray, spray, screw, sprinkle, sicker, prescribe, prisoner, exclaim, exclusive, prosper, gospel, plausible, explicit, extreme, explore, cider, sober, sable, sidle, sickle, string, disclose, physical, satchel, scrawl, scrawny, descry, discourage, scribe, scratch, extremely, expressly, extra, dishonor, civility, struggle, spray, spruce, stretch, stretcher, struggle, scraper, scribble, splasher, suffer, civil, cipher, gastric, pastry, bicycle, disclaim, descry, discourage, discourse, discursive, disgrace.

REVIEW EXERCISE NO. 4.

Double and Triple Consonants. Pages 42-49.

Write in shorthand, without referring to the previous lessons: Play, pray, flow, fro, side, cider, sad, sadder, saddle, sick, sickly, ply, pry, grow, glow, flee, free, flame, frame, muffle, title, tackle, pickle, bushel, official, author, oval, offer, freckle, struggle, upper, utter, keeper, couple, ruffle, manner, tanner, flag, flake, floor, flurry, flowery, shriek, shrub, plaster, blister, probe, broom, break, drop, plague, labor, press, breeze, brook, eagle, gross, travel, measure, display, displease, sister,

(OVER)

discourage, disgrace, civil, bicycle, disclaim, throw, civility, gospel, exclaim, exclusive, extremely, expressly, physical, plausible, explicit, stretcher, title, subscribe, describe, disclose, scribe, scribble, cycle, extra, dishonor, plumber, label, Friday, special, prosper, pastry, cipher, suffer, deceiver, commerce, taper, able, signer, supreme, enclosure, plainer, explosive, stream, sprinkle, fluffy, initial, young, vapor, brace, supper, freely, crime, disagreeable, ample, disable, supercede, essential, yet, any, him, visible, sober, cable, cheaper, were, usual, supremacy, stifle, freeze, descry, spray, spruce, flog, commercial, bottle, former, extremity, explosive, major, close, cloister, shrug, battle, shrimp, clay, gale, gray, pale, pressure, level, with, was, labor, suppress, civilize, grace, favor, disable, frozen, fable, splice, praise, supple, distress, dinner, miner, sooner, cloy, Oliver, Frazier, Harrisburg, Liverpool, Troy, Buffalo.

Blame no one for the official error. The disagreeable task will discourage the boy. The package came by express to my address. He will give them fair measure.

<h2 style="text-align:center">EXERCISE XVII.</h2>

<h3 style="text-align:center">THE n HOOK. PAR. 152 TO 157.</h3>

Pain, pen, pin, pun, bun, boon, spoon, spawn, Spain, ten, den, din, down, thrown, frown, drown, moan, tone, cone, loan, men, skein, throne, alone, bean, dean, hewn, broken, token, blacken, sudden, stone, brandy, ran, run, roan, brine, spine, plenty, clean, hone, penny, pony, rain, rainy, piano, prune, plain, refrain, bone, bony, join, pine, coin, crown, Jane, cleanly, screening, joining, moaning, fan, van, fancy, vanish, banish, punish, plan, shrine, occupancy, replenish, clemency, vagrancy, tune, bane, deign.

dawn, prone, drawn, drown, keen, crane, spleen, sprain, strain, chin, chain, gin, green, grain, grown, feign, flown, frown, even, oven, thin, then, shown, lean, lawn, mine, known, clannish.

EXERCISE XVIII.

THE *f* OR *v* HOOK AND *s* ADDED TO FINAL HOOKS.

Par. 158 *to* 166.

Pave, drove, crave, ruff, cuff, drive, prove, Jove, cough, rebuff, proving, bluff, dive, dove, divinity, heave, believe, cove, cave, grave, grove, chief, chaff, rough, hive, strive, gruff, cleave, cliff, tiff, stuff, puffs, paves, craves, drives, duns, tuns, tins, dens, pains, gains, cleans, cleaves, groans, stones, strives, drones, drowns, crowns, feigns, shines, mines, moans, shuns, glance, glances, pounce, pounces, danced, pounced, punster, fence, fences, evinces, hive, hove, serve, deserve, bereave, reserve, coffee, taffy, huffy, defy, survey, gravy, Java, proves, braves, cloves, paves, strives, calves, proofs, define, devoid, divide, devote, graphic, pins, spans, tones, strains, trains, drains, sprains, joins, fans, frowns, veins, lines, means, vines, lancer, cancer, fencing, ransom, lonesome, princes, prances, bounces, chances.

EXERCISE XIX.

WORD-SIGNS AND PHRASES.

Par. 167 *and* 168.

Key to Phrases on page 54.

1. That-the, for-the, in-the, have-the, think-the, of-the, to-the, on-the, should-the, all-the, by-the, if-the.

2. Are-the, from-the, was-the, during-the, until-the, till-the, which-the, ought-the, owe-the, or-the, but-the, value-the.

3. And-for-a, and-for-the, and-have-a, and-have-the, and-that-a, and-when-a, or-a, but-a, on-a, should-a, of-a.

4. And-is, and-as, is-a, as-a, is-the, as-the, and-is-the, and-as-the, and-is-a, and-as-a.

Principal, principally, principle, practice, member, remember, remembered, number, numbered, truth, doctor, dear, during, tell, till, until, care, call, difficult, difficulty, Mr., remark, remarkable, more, near, nor, full, fully, from, every, very, value, three, there, their, other, sure, surely, pleasure.

The principal thing to remember in this work is that we must practice each lesson faithfully. To tell-the truth Dr. Smith will call there no more until he is sure that-the difficulty has been taken away. We shall have-the pleasure of listening to remarks from Mr. Brown. There were three pails full of milk very near the other door. Value your time; it-is money. Their names are dear to-the people. Take care to call things by their right names. It will surely give me pleasure to call there with you. Tell him to go home till noon. There-are many other plans for study during-the week. We fully perceive the difficulty, but-the truth is until you care more for work than for pleasure there surely will-be few chances for us to help you. Every chair in-the room, and there-are many, is of small value, but of dear cost. Very many people preach principles; very few practice. Dear Dr. Green took care of Mr. Mason during his illness. Until you care to call things by their right names you-will-have difficulty with everything you try to explain. We usually have no difficulty in obtaining the names of-a number of-the principal members of-the House.

REVIEW EXERCISE NO. 5.

THE *n* HOOK, THE *f* OR *v* HOOK, CIRCLES ADDED TO HOOKS,
WORD-SIGNS. PAGES 50-57.

Write in shorthand without referring to the previous lessons: Pain, pave, feign, stain, strain, strive, strains, strives, thrown, frown, broken, plenty, brandy, believe, divide, chances, lonesome, pen, penny, cough, coffee, bereave, brave, bluff, cleave, drives, graphic, divinity, remain, sermon, replenish, blacken, taken, engrave, prefix, blown, green, refrain, refine, refiner, refinery, ravine, preference, serve, survey, rain, rainy, deaf, defy, chief, achieve, morning, earn, arena, occupancy, drowns, danced, alone, tune, feigns, rough, shown, define, crave, oven, proof, chances, sudden, tuns, splasher, plenty, cliff, lawn, lawns, strives, explain, expense, many, declines, defeat, disclose, nine, financial, soften, deserves, cloves, refrain, token, known, exclusive, spoon, run, runs, vain, chains, thin, visible, again, glances, refer, cyclone, down, fleecy, reprove, doves, residence, retains, plan, disagree, spray, money, man, iron, gone, grief, grieves, assign, restrains, roofs, coupons, shuns, fans, fencing, vanish, chaff, gruff, ransom, skein, evinces, explore, fences, settle, leisure, commercial, blacken, even, moan, many, grain, grains, possible, cypress, legal, farmer, thrice, screening, join, finish, suppress, seven, feasible, references, response, extra, staff, approves, rains, observes, Brown, Boston, Dayton, Henry, David, Arkansas, Kansas, Maine, Michigan.

The iron wheel of the machine is broken. To define a dream we say it is an idle fancy that passes through the brain in sleep. She will devote an hour each day to the study of music and will divide the remaining time into periods of two hours each for the study of other branches.

EXERCISE XX.

THE LARGE *wa* HOOK.

Par. 169 *to* 175.

Twain, tweak, twig, twin, twist, dwell, dwarf, queen, queer, quest, quick, quiver, quiz, square, squall, squaw, squeak, squeeze, squeal, quail, quince, quack, bequest, inquest, quibble, twill, twitch, twinkle, quarrel, quota, quoth, quiet, equip, equity, iniquity, anguish.

Ml, Nl, Rl, AND *Lr.*

Par. 176 *to* 179.

Learn, peril, panel, ferule, collar, color, final, gallery, family, channel, carol, pommel, tunnel, animal, mackerel, melancholy, relapse, relative, lurch, neuralgia, scholar, rural, spiral, barrel, ferrule, camel, enamel, funnel, scholars, barrels.

EXERCISE XXI.

THE LARGE FINAL HOOKS AND *S-shun* CURL.

Par. 180 *to* 188.

Mission, motion, nation, profession, caution, auction, action, session, oration, provision, addition, edition, duration, location, locomotion, notion, daughter, brother, cater, bother, gather, writer, station, rations, passion, patience, creation, twitter, trotter, blotter, stutter, scatter, cheater, pleader, platter, chatter, clatter, glitter, director, educator, secretion, decision, position, disposition, physician, dispossession, operation, operators, sensation, sensational, transition, transitional, involution, evolution, execution, exaction, exertion, exposition, expression, magician, mutation, narration, proposition, commission, adoption, option, cushion, implication, reaction, application, nation, mention, animation, invasion, revision, elevation, pollution, dictionary, educational, actions, occupations, fashions, visions, sections, position, opposition, supposition, precision, accession, civilization, accusation, dispensation, ocean, shun, shuns, oceans.

EXERCISE XXII.

THE HALVING PRINCIPLE.

Par. 189 to 195.

Bake, baked, tap, tapped, dip, dipped, rub, rubbed, brag, bragged, lame, lamed, pay, paid, east, not, mite, let, lave, laved, bought, taught, save, saved, glad, mad, bad, crude, nailed, mailed, sent, send, blood, proud, cloud, papered, better, brief, briefest, laid, old, debt, made, street, sprite, measured, bathed, met, made, claimed, get, crept, played, prayed, doubled, troubled, flight, fright, spread, displayed, brood, bred, bled, trade, grade, supply, supplied, pinched, banished, touched, tacked, tracked, vouched, slipped, nipped, pegged, paged, plugged, pledged, drugged, begged, apt, wept, walked, oft, aft, east, etched, ached, art, eased, oozed, cheat, chat, cat, cut, feat, fit, fat, nut, night, note, mite, meet, vied, void, vowed, viewed, end, need, nod, needle, sound, sand, sinned, signed, hired, heard, hard, hemmed, meddle, muddle, middle, elocutionist, bravest, roughest, vainest, finest, oftenest, peopled, labored, baffled.

EXERCISE XXIII.

THE HALVING PRINCIPLE (Continued).

Par. 196 to 204.

Bent, bend, pent, penned, dived, paved, caution, cautioned, stationed, fined, mined, drift, moaned, frowned, approved, drafts, craved, glitter, glittered, round, around, grieved, plant, rent, words, earned, prints, splints, bends, tents, joints, mound, mountain, throned, shrined, remained, act, acted, ended, protected, treated, dreaded, freighted, heaved, hotel, wilds, fiat, poet, looked, sentiment, sometimes, fact, evoked, pity, estimate, root, tarried, defendant, superintendent, vacate, windy, hired, mitigate, tidy, mud, muddy, heaved, laid, red, ready, did, dado, create, windy, locked, beautify, effected, pawned, spend, sprained, trained, twined, gained, drained, friend, cleaned, paved, grieved, grooved, achieved, motioned, fashioned, pits, pets, cheats, chats, fits, skates, sheets, fleets, shouts, fights, thoughts, streets, grades, deeds, coined, scant, scanned, grand, ground, tended, sounded, petted, lighted, alphabet, credit, freedom, raft, rained, raved, roved, served, surround, fared, named, fired, feared.

EXERCISE XXIV.

The Doubling Principle and Special Vocalization.

Par. 205 to 214.

Feather, mother, thither, father, smother, smoother, neither, another, weather, shatter, flutter, Easter, flatter, oyster, letter, loiter, smatter, slaughter, meter, center, winter, niter, water, motor, alter, laughter, tender, tinder, order, fodder, shudder, surrender, gender, tinker, anchor, franker, clinker, hanker, rancor, finger, hunger, younger, temper, scamper, hamper, damper, distemper, amber, timber, limber, lumber, December, feathers, fingers, tempers, tampers, northern, alternation.

Believe, charm, scarlet, marble, skill, dark, regard, gold, skull, Turkey, journal, scourge, court, curve, secure.

REVIEW EXERCISE NO. 6.

LARGE INITIAL AND FINAL HOOKS, S-SHUN CURL, THE HALV-
ING PRINCIPLE, THE DOUBLING PRINCIPLE. PAGES 57-67.

Write in shorthand without referring to the previous lessons: Twig, queer, quick, squeak, squeal, learn, panel, channel, family, mission, nation, session, location, bother, writer,
rubbed, paid, bought, bend, paved, cautioned, mother, father,
brother, neither, dwell, quest, collar, tunnel, provision, passion,
chatter, sent, send, bread, trade, measured, drift, drafts, letter,
winter, smother, loiter, final, gallery, queen, patience, scatter,
edition, position, decision, made, debt, papered, round, around,
joints, center, shudder, earned, words, square, quack, barrels,
animal, quiet, flight, fright, brood, pledged, east, cushion,
application, achieved, acted, protected, dreaded, estimate,
laughter, tender, believe, turkey, sometimes, surrender,
served, alphabet, equip, bequest, relative, disposition, physician,
sensation, journal, cheats, defendant, heard, dictionary, inquest,
scholar, educator, involution, execution, exposition, finest,
streets, tended, rained, temper, hamper, lumber, revision,
occupations, quoth, iniquity, enamel, ferrule, exertion, expression, adoption, vacate, proposition, bravest, elocutionist, December, younger, finger, middle, supposition, educational, melancholy, anguish, visions, friend, spend, cleaned, alteration,
needle, accession, surround, freedom, credit, walked, feathers,
motioned, merit, sentiment, peopled, dispensation, sensational,
spiral, accusation, pinched, roughest, sprained, timber,
September, Easter, thoughts, mitigate, funnel, magician,
platter, twitter, sound, fined, mountain, bound, northern,
civilization.

EXERCISE XXV.

WORD-SIGNS AND PHRASES

Page 68.

Opinion, upon, been, general, generally, before, whatever, different, difference, can, begin, begun, began, govern, governed, government, influence, information, United States, object, objected, objection, subject, subjected, subjection, several, knowledge, acknowledge, represent, representative, representation, should-be, that-they, has-been, it-has-been, which-has-been.

His information upon-the subject was wide ; his influence with-the government, great. The subject under discussion was-the effect upon-the United States government, of taxation without representation. Before you begin to object to this method of work show that your general knowledge, at least, is good. Whatever difference of opinion they held upon other subjects, the representatives all agreed upon this. You generally begin several pieces of work before finishing any. There is much difference in meaning between *subject* and *object* as-well-as between *subjection* and *objection*. A large representation came before the House and offered several objections to-the bill. His general knowledge, and his information upon all matters pertaining to-the United States government were acknowledged. They represent several different societies by their dress. Whatever they began they finished. His opinion upon all subjects was prized because of his extended knowledge.

EXERCISE XXVI.

HALF-LENGTH WORD-SIGNS.

Page 70.

Particular, particularly, part, profit, prophet, spirit, build, billed, board, behind, told, toward, child, gentlemen, gentleman, quite, could, accord, according, accordingly, accurate, cared, called, good, after, future, afford, that, without, short, assured, astonish, astonished, astonishment, establish, established, establishment, immediate, immediately, somewhat, nature, under, hundred.

After doing quite accurate work they could not afford to make-a hundred errors. The child was told particularly that it was done for his future good. The establishment of-a Board of Directors assured much profit to-the gentlemen of-the association. The time was somewhat short, and they accordingly called on-the Board to build the house immediately. They could not afford to-be behind-the spirit of-the times. A particular part of-the profit went to build the church. He told-the gentleman his account was quite accurate. He cared not to-be called good, and was quite astonished that he should-be. After much discussion they decided to establish a firm in-the near future. Not without astonishment, he assured me that he was in no immediate need. There are a hundred things in nature that interest and astonish us. The establishment was somewhat short of money, after-a good financial year. That part of-the profit you can afford to-do without, in-the future.

EXERCISE XXVII.

PREFIXES AND AFFIXES

Par. 215 *to* 229.

Condense, contain, condition, considerable, command, commence, unconfined, accompany, recommend, recognize, decompose, accommodation, contravene, countermand, contraband, conquest, consent, concern, conditions, self-respect, self-same, self-made, self-possessed, enslave, inspiration, instruct, instruction, instrument, insult, insulation, magnify, magnitude, magnificence, circumscribe, circumflex, circumvent, circumspect, doing, engraving, meaning, drifting, craving, trying, contractor, buying, stability, friendship, hardship, township, legibility, doings, tidings, forever, whenever, myself, yourself, themselves, successful, painful, sleeping, profitable, peculiarity, unseemly, inconvenient, counterfeit, instrumentality, ourselves, herself, gazing, compensation, admissible, compact, compare, compass, compassion, complement, complete, complex, compose, compromise, concave, conceal, conceit, conceive, concession, conclusion, recommence, recompense, incomplete, reconcile, reconstruct, recognition, controversy, counteraction, countermarch, countersign, self-acting, self-assertion, self-command, self-defense, abusing, accusing, etchings, buildings, himself, thyself, punctuality, stability prosperity.

EXERCISE XXVIII.

WORD-SIGNS.

Page 74.

Opportunity, dollar, had, advertise, advertisement, much, large, larger, bill, balance, deliver, delivered, delivery, correct, corrected, character, aware, public, publish, published, publication, ever, however, never, nevertheless, notwithstanding, assure, million, matter, now, first, important, importance, improve, improvement, impossible, impossibility, this, those, thank, thousand, though.

They had-a good opportunity to advertise in-a much larger paper. The corrected account showed a balance of one dollar in our favor. He delivered a speech on public characters. It-is next to impossible to attend to matters of great importance now; nevertheless there-will-be an effort to-do so. I assure you that neither a thousand nor a million dollars could ever tempt him to-do wrong. That-it-will-be impossible to-do this is certain notwithstanding the fact of-its great importance. He did not thank the gentleman though he had-a good opportunity. Those are matters of importance; never neglect them. The first bill of goods delivered, though large, was correct. The character of-the publication is now much improved. Are-you aware that in-such-a case as you-mention there-will-be-a larger bill than we wish-to pay. This opportunity to advertise may never occur again. The first address was on-the importance of-a good character. His manners were much improved by his opportunities.

Material for Practice.

As has been already said, to become proficient in writing shorthand requires an immense amount of practice. The material on the following pages is given for this purpose; not as being sufficient but to show the kind of matter that should be selected, and to start the student in the right way. The words have been counted and the figures after each letter or article, indicate the number of words therein. They are also divided into groups of twenty-five words by the accent mark. Words connected by the hyphen are to be phrased when written in shorthand. Difficult outlines or phrases are explained in the foot-notes, either by reference to some preceding paragraph or by indicating, by the use of type, what shorthand characters should be used. In this latter method, all *stroke consonants* are represented by *capitals* and the *circles, loops, hooks,* and *other appendages,* by *small letters.* When a stroke is to be written upward, a *large italic* is used. The position of the outline is denoted by the figures 1, 2, 3. The same matter will also be found in shorthand, beginning on page 148.

These exercises should first be written slowly, care being taken to use the proper characters and to execute them perfectly. Then write the same matter over *hundreds* of times, each time writing correctly and a little faster than before. *Read your notes after each writing and observe and correct any inaccuracies.*

The following marks may be used in punctuating:

×or / period. ? or × interrogation. ! × exclamation. ～～～ or ┵ dash. ※ asterisk. ⁋ paragraph. ( ) parenthesis.

= hyphen, ⸋ capital. laughter. cheers.

Business Letters.

ADVERTISING.

DEAR-SIR: —

Having applied at-the New-York office of-your agents for-the advertisement (of the)[1] interest on-the bonds (of the) Chesapeake[2] &' Ohio R. R. Co.[3], payable on-the 2nd prox., and-having-been referred to-you, I would-respectfully request a-copy for-the columns of-this' paper.

"The Sun" is universally[4] admitted to-be-the-most trustworthy-and instructive chronicle of-all[5] matters relating to-the money market, and-most incorporated' companies use-its columns to announce meetings, elections, and-dividend and-interest notices.

Mailed herewith is-a copy of "The Sun" for-your convenient scrutiny.' Trusting to-receive-a favorable reply, I-am,

Very-respectfully-yours, (111).

BANKING.

DEAR-SIR: —

Your-favor[6] (of the) 18th inst. is received with inquiry for-the standing, etc., of John Jones, of-this-city.[7]

Mr. Jones does'-not keep his personal account with-this-bank, and-I-am-not sufficiently informed in-regard to his matters to-make-a statement about them.' Personally he-is-in' good standing here, and-all-the business we-have-done with-him has-been attended to promptly and to-our entire' satisfaction.

Yours-respectfully, (78).

---

1. *Of-the* indicated by proximity. See 283.
2. *Chesapeake.* CH²-sP-K.
3. *R. R. Co.* See 266.
4. *Universally,* N-Vrs²-L.
5. *Of-all,* VL.
6. *Your-favor,* Y²-Vr.
7. *Of-this-city.* See 265.
8. *He-is-in,* hsN¹.

BOOK PUBLISHING.

DEAR-SIR: —

We-have-your-favor (of the) 27th ultimo, and-enclose circulars of-some of-our best selling atlases. We should like to arrange' with you to handle our publications exclusively and-permanently in-your county the coming season.

Our New Indexed Atlas (of the) World[9] is-a first-class' publication and-is meeting with-a large sale in-all[10] parts (of the) country. The retail prices are at-least[11] 25 per cent. lower-than[12] those' asked for-works of corresponding value on-the market. Our General Atlas (of the) World has-been made to answer-the demand for-a low-priced,' household work. Anyone can sell our Pocket Atlas and-some agents, working on-the larger atlases, carry it as-a side issue for quick sale' where nothing-else [13] can-be-sold. Already 500,000 copies have-been sold and-we-think-it-will last for-several years.

We can' give-you exclusive control of-a reasonable amount of territory on any (of the) above publications, excepting-the[14] Pocket Atlas. Of-this-book we-do'-not keep any record, but let anyone who applies sell it. We can supply you any or all of-the above publications at 33⅓ per cent.' discount from retail prices, and-if-you wish-to examine samples before ordering stock, shall-be-pleased to forward same at net price. We supply'-the agent with everything necessary for learning-the business and-starting-the canvass.

Everything seems to point to-a lively business for-the coming season.' Our salesmen in-all parts (of the) country are sending in very encouraging reports and-all seem to-be-

---

9. *World*, w *R²-L*d.
10. *In-all.* See 273.
11. *At-least*, Tlst¹.
12. *Lower-than*, *L²-*Rn.

13. *Nothing-else*, N-TH²-NG-Ls.
14. *Excepting-the.* See 223.

pleased with-the prospects.   Recently one' of-our salesmen reported selling twenty-one copies of-our New Indexed Atlas (of the) World in-six-days. We-hope-you-will
conclude to " hitch' horses " with-us.[15]

Very-truly, (305).

BOOTS AND SHOES.

DEAR-SIR: —

We-are-in-receipt (of the) goods which-you return and-
credit them on-your-account, with-the-exception of ½ doz.
Waukenphasts' and 1-6 doz. French Kid, which were dam-
aged so they could-not-be returned to-our stock.   We-are
compelled to-sell odd lots like' these at $4.00 per doz., when-
we can find-a customer, and-we could-not allow-you more-
than[16] that amount. You-can, no'-doubt, sell them out
with less loss than we could, and-we-have-no-objection to-
your making-a reduced price, provided you do-not' advertise them or sell them in-such (a) way as-to cause others
to think-you-are cutting prices on-our regular[17] goods.

We-would' gladly allow-you more if we could get more
for-them, but we cannot and-prefer not to-receive-them
even at-this price. We' hold the ½ doz. subject to-your
order, and-you-will-please inform us at-once[18] what disposition to-make of same.   By doing so' you-will greatly
oblige,

Yours-truly, (181).

ELECTRICAL APPARATUS.

DEAR-SIR: —

Replying to-your enclosed request dated the 11th and
asking for quotations on three " communicators," we-think-

---

15. *With-us.* See 277.   17. *Regular,* R'-G.
16. *More-than.* See 272.   18. *At-once.* See p. 96. line 11.

there-is[19] some error in writing'-the name (of the) article, and would suggest that-your people probably require commutators,[20] as there-is-no part of-an electrical[21] plant called-a' communicator.

If-it is[22] commutators that are required, kindly obtain for-us the size (of the) dynamo upon-which they-are-to-be used, and'-we-shall-be-pleased to quote you prices on receipt-(of) your reply.

Yours-very-truly, (91).

FURNITURE.

GENTLEMEN: —

We send-you to day, by-mail, photograph of Chamber Suit which contains ten pieces; namely, Bedstead, Dresser, Wash-stand, Table, Four Chairs, Rocker, and Towel'-Rack. These we-have finished in imitation mahogany and antique ash; price we make to-you $22.50. We consider this an excellent' good value, and-have-made-the margin close in hopes that-you-will-be-able-to give-us-an order. We-have four in antique' ash and-two in imitation mahogany, with more coming.

When you-are through with-the photograph, kindly return to-us, and oblige,

Yours-truly, (99).

GRAIN.

DEAR-SIR: —

Replying to-your esteemed-favor (of the) 21st inst., will-say that-we quote you on-the basis of to-day's market the following' prices, which-are[23] subject to change as-the market advances or declines.

---

19. *We-think-there-is.* See 270. 21. *Electrical,* L²-K-Tr-Kl.
20. *Commutators,* com dot- 22. *If-it-is,* Fts¹.
    Ttrs². 23. *Which-are,* CHr².

No. 2 corn, 64½ cts.; high mixed corn, 66 cts.; No. 2 white' oats, 44 cts. These prices are for delivery to Boston points, South Framingham included.

We send-you-by to-day's mail samples of-our coarse and' fine feed meal and cracked corn, which we-will-sell you at $1.35 per hundred, sacks included. Enclosed you-will-find samples' of yellow granulated meal and white bolted meal. We-will-sell the former at $1.45 in sacks delivered in New-York, via' West Shore Road; sacks 6 cts. extra. The white bolted meal will cost you $1.35 for-same delivery.

Please let-us-know' by return mail if-you-can use any of-the goods specified above. If so, by sending us your order, you-will greatly oblige,

Yours'-very-truly, (177).

HARDWARE.

DEAR-SIR: –

We-have-yours of yesterday and-have received-a cable-gram[24] from our London friends accepting your offer for sheets. We-have-no intention' whatever of sending-you anything except-the exact make and exact quality (of the) one ton of sheets which-you-received last month by S. S.' *Noordland;* and-we guarantee to supply, in-every-way and respect, the same quality and-make.

If-that one ton proved satisfactory, as you say' it did, there-will-be no question about-the suitability (of the) steel. Should-it not turn[25] out exactly as per sample ship-ment, we-are' ready to assume all-the consequences. We-think-that you-will-find this guarantee perfectly sufficient.

We-must, of-course, also have-some assurance from'-you that-you-will work-the steel the same-as-you did before, so-as-to produce similar results.

Awaiting-the favor of-your reply', we remain,

Yours-truly, (154).

---

24. *Cablegram,* K-Bl²-Gr-M.   25. *Turn,* T²-Rn.

HEATING.

DEAR-SIR: —

For-the consideration (of the) sum of one hundred eighty-six dollars and seventy-five cents ($186.75), we-will furnish, deliver, and set up complete in'-your house in Sayville, L. I., one No. 44 Richardson's Cyclone, portable, gastight, re-vertible flue furnace.   We-will furnish and set six new register boxes' as indicated on diagram. We-will provide and put up all hot air pipes in-the cellar, chimneys, etc., neces-sary to connect-the furnace with'-the registers in-a safe and-proper manner.   Also provide and put up for-the furnace a heavy galvanized iron, smoke pipe, with patent draft' regulator.   We-are to-do all mason's and tinman's work, setting up the furnace and-fixtures as specified complete and ready for use, and-will' give-you a strictly first-class job in-every-respect.   We-will guarantee-the furnace to-be of sufficient capacity to warm the rooms to-a' temperature of 70 degrees in-the coldest weather.

Upon acceptance (of the) above proposition, we-will-be-pleased to submit to-you a plan for' heating the house, showing-the manner of putting in-the pipes, etc.   It-is de-sirable to-have-an understanding how the work is-to-be'-done, before-the work is commenced.

Very-respectfully submitted, (209)

INSURANCE.

DEAR-SIR: —

You have doubtless seen newspaper account (of the) burning (of the) American Excelsior Mills, Rochester, N.-Y., yesterday morning, on-which-the UNION' had-a policy of $4,000 under No. 47,861.

Referring to daily report, you-will observe the rate was reduced to 2' per cent. The reason for-this large reduction in rate was that-the plant had-been thoroughly equipped with automatic sprinklers, and-in-the judgment (of' the)

Factory-Committee (of the) State of New-York, Board of Underwriters, the additional protection warranted this reduction. As you-are-aware, we-have-never' suffered-a serious attack of-this sprinkler craze, having held to-the conservative view that until-their utility had-been thoroughly established, it-was-the' part of wisdom to give our companies the benefit of any doubt we-might entertain on-the subject. For-this reason we declined to increase' our line, contenting ourselves with-the line already written.

While at-this writing I-have-no particulars as-to-the origin (of the) fire, the' total destruction of-some 65 per cent. (of the) entire plant is evidence to-the fact that-the sprinklers were of no practical value.

I-enclose' herewith diagram (of the) works. Fire originated in-the machine building, No. 6, which, together with Nos. 9, 12, and 15, was totally destroyed, unless' it-be-a small salvage on No. 12.

Respectfully, (234).

REGARDING INVESTMENT.

DEAR-SIR:—

Please find herewith enclosed note for $600 and-deed of-trust on eighty acres of land in Stafford County, Kansas, a'-very choice loan which I-have selected for-you. Please also find enclosed draft on New-York for $17.15, the same being' interest on-the Robbins loan to Sept. 1, 1892, from which date your new loan bears interest. I-have examined quite-a number of' loans and-have at-last[26] selected this as-a particularly good one, with-which I-am-sure you-will-be-pleased.

If-you have any' more money that-you care to invest, I-think I-can get-you other loans at-(the) same-rate, seven per cent. for five years.'

Respectfully, (126).

---

26. *At-last*, Tlst[3].

LEATHER.

Dear-Sir: —

We-have-your-favor (of the) 27th and-now enclose invoice of-our shipment of No. 537 in-the lightest substance that'-we make, as you ordered.   We have-no hesitation in saying, that for durability and permanency of color and gloss, this leather cannot-be excelled.'   We should-be happy to-have-your orders on any (of the) grades.   We put them up at 28, 26, 24, and 22 cents, also' in large skins at 22, 20, 18, and 15 cents.   We also send-you to-day the two dozens of extra choice stock ordered.   Believe you'-will-find them to meet your wants.

Regarding the No. 585 stock cracking, would-say-that while you-may find an occasional skin do'-so, it-is-not-the character (of the) stock.   You-will-find this in Patna. skins once in-a while and-it-cannot-be detected' from-the appearance (of the) skins.   We-are selling this stock largely and-have-no-other complaint; we, therefore, think that-you-may-be a'-little unduly alarmed.   Of-course, we-do-not wish-to urge anything on-you, that might be at-all a-disappointment, but-you know Patna' stock is treacherous at best.   Still, we-think-you-will-find the leather gives good service.   Shall-be-glad to-have-your orders, either on' these or on other goods in-our line.

Yours-respectfully, (235).

LEGAL.

GENTLEMEN : —

Regarding-the matter of-your claim against Smith & Brown, we-would-say that-this claim was put in suit and-is still undecided'.   We-have sued E. Smith and N. Brown, alleging that-they-were doing business together as partners.   Mr. Brown is-a man of-large wealth' and-is able to pay all the accounts against himself and Smith but he denies that-he-was-a partner in the concern.

There were' quite-a number of suits commenced against these parties in-(the)-same-way, and-at-the spring term of-our court it-was agreed, among'-the various attorneys, to-refer-the case to-a referee and-have one-case, at-least, tried before him to settle-the point as-to' whether Brown was-a partner or not. The case has-not-been heard yet, so-the matter is still undecided and-will-probably be for'-some-time, as-it[27] will undoubtedly go to-the Supreme Court (of the) State.

If we can prove that Brown was-a partner, there-will'-be no difficulty about collecting-the full amount of your claim, but-as Smith is worth nothing, if-we cannot prove that, the claim will'-be worthless. We-will advise you as-soon-as a-decision in-the-matter is reached.

Yours-truly, (218).

LEGISLATIVE.

DEAR-SIR:—

Your-favor of-recent-date has-been received-and would have-been answered sooner, but for my absence in-New-York until-the' recent session (of the) Legislature.

The Legislative Record is published this session, but so far-as I know, the State printers printed copies sufficient for'-the Legislature only, but do-not-know-that they-have any arrangement to-send single copies, by-mail, to-others. I-will look into-the' matter, however, and-if-it-is-possible, will-have it sent to-you. At Washington, the Congressional Record is sent to any-one who subscribes' for-it. Last year, I-remember, I-had-it sent-to me here in Albany, during-the session.

It-is-not true, as reported, that' I-intend introducing-a bill to annex the town of Westchester to-the city of New-York. At-least I would-not feel free to'-do-so, unless

---

27. *As-it*, Zt'.

backed up by-a petition signed by-a considerable ma-
jority (of the) tax-payers of-your town. With-such action
back of-me', I would, of-course, be-able-to consider-the
matter in-a favorable light.   I-have-heard, in-New-York,
however, that such-a bill' will-probably be introduced by-a
city member.   I-intend to keep track of-it and-will send
copies to-you and-to-the newspapers' of-your town, as-
soon-as the bill is printed.

I-have-not-yet received-your circular regarding-the State
R. R. Commissioners.   I-am-very' much in earnest in my
effort to promote any reasonable bill which-will give-the
Commissioners more power than they now possess.   At-
present, they'-are little more-than clerks to-do-the bidding
of-their superiors.

Very-truly, (289).

LUMBER.

DEAR-SIR : —

Replying to-your-favor (of the) 10th inst., we regret to
learn that, through-the disinclination (of the) Erie railroad
to accommodate us', you were unable to carry out the arrangement made by Mr. Johnson, with regard to-the un-
loading and-disposition (of the) portion (of the) Dock'-
Department[28] order referred to.

If-the Dock-Department will-not accept the four sticks
12x12, have-the stevedore[29] put-the timber into-the' water
at 57th St., together with any-other portion (of the) cargo
for-that Department that may-be rejected; and-let the
sticks so rejected' be firmly rafted and secured at-the-foot
of 57th St. in-such-(a)-manner that-they will-not-get away,
until further disposition (of' the) same can-be-made. Have-
the kindness to give-this-matter your personal-and careful

---

28. Sec 266.   29. *Stevedore*, sTv¹-D-R.

attention, and arrange with-the stevedore for-the cost' of-this-work, making as-good-a bargain as you-can with-him and-we will see that-the-amount is paid.

The Department will', undoubtedly, take-the balance of-their portion (of the) cargo as-fast-as you-can discharge it.

Yours-truly, (194).

RAILROAD.

DEAR-SIR: —

Rate of $45.00 on-the horses from Syracuse, N.-Y., to Springfield, Mass., via our-route, would-not-be profitable. If we'-had plenty of rolling stock so-that our stock cars would, at any-time of-the year, be liable to-be idle, we could better' take-up the question with-the C. Vt. R.-R.

You-should-not load hay on-the depot platform. It-is directly contrary to-the rules', and-the Company would-be liable for-all[30] damage done in-case-of fire.

We-will later take-up the question of cattle suit.

Very'-truly, (101).

REAL ESTATE.

DEAR-SIR: —

On-the 30th day of September, 1889, the Kinderhook & Hudson Railway-Company paid-you $175 for right of'-way over-your premises and-took-a warranty deed for-(the)-same, free-and clear from all incumbrances, but-the records show that-there-is'-a mortgage made by-yourself to Matthew Foster for $2,500, dated May 1st, 1884, and recorded May 8th, 1884', in Book of Mortgages No. 60, page 590.

Is-this mortgage paid? If so, will-you please send me the satisfaction, so-that' I-can-have-it recorded? If-not, will-you see Mr. Foster and-have-a release of-these premises from-the operation of-this mortgage' executed?

An-immediate reply will oblige,

Yours-truly, (133).

---

30. *For-all*, Fl².

Testimony.

SUPREME COURT OF NEW YORK.

EDWARD W. SMITH

vs.

PETER JOHNSON.

James M. Fisher, being duly sworn, testifies on behalf (of the) plaintiff, as-follows':

Direct examination by Mr. Wheeler:

Q.[31] What-is your name?   A. James M. Fisher.

Q. How-old are-you?   A. I-am 23 years-(of')-age.

Q. Where-do-you-reside?   A. I-reside in-the city of Baltimore, Md.

Q. What-is your business?   A. I-am an auctioneer' by occupation.

Q. Do-you-know-the parties to-this-action, plaintiff and defendant?   A. I-am-acquainted with Mr. Edward W. Smith. I-am'-not personally acquainted with Mr. Peter Johnson.

Q. Are-you acquainted with Richard F. Mason? A. I-am.

---

31. Questions and answers should be indicated in the transcript by " Q." and "A." It is not, however, necessary to write these letters in the original notes, but all questions may be commenced at the extreme left edge of the paper, and all answers about one inch from the left edge. If the questions and answers are very short, they may be put on the same line, leaving considerable space between.

Q. When-did-you become acquainted with'-him and-where? A. I-became acquainted with-him in April, 1891, in-the city of Baltimore, Md.

Q. Did-you enter into-the' employ of, or-make any business arrangement or connection with-said-Mason? A. Yes,-sir.

Q. State when, where, and what brought it about? A. I'-went into his employ sometime in April, 1889, in-the city of Baltimore. I-entered into his employ at-the instigation of-my'-father. My-father became acquainted with Mr.-Mason at-the office (of the) City Detectives[32] in-the City Hall. Mr.-Mason asked Mr. Fred Wilson', also a-detective at that-time, if-he-could find-a good-man for-his-business, and-my-father told-him (Mason) that-his son' was out-of business and-was seeking employment.

Q. State what-was-the-nature (of the) business of-said-Mason? A. He-was in-the' tea-and coffee business.

Q. In what-capacity were-you employed? A. I-was employed as-a salesman.

Q. State where-you-entered upon-your' employment? A. I-entered on my employment in-the city of Baltimore.

Q. How long did-you continue with-him? A. I continued with-him' about three years.

Q. Did-your employment involve your traveling from-place-to-place[33] with-said-Mason? A. It did involve my traveling from-place'-to-place.

Q. State in regular order the-places you went to, and-the periods of-time spent in-the various places, so far-as'-you-can remember-them. (A. I-spent ten weeks in Baltimore; from-there I-went with-him to Philadelphia and-stayed about three-months'; from-there I-went with-him to Harrisburgh, Pa., and-stayed there one week; from-there I-went with-him to Washington, D. C., and'-stayed there

32. *Detectives*, Dt²-Kt-Vs.   33. *From-place-to-place.* See 284.

about ten weeks; from-there I-went with-him to Detroit, Mich., and-stayed there about one month; from-there I-went to' Chicago with-him and-stayed there about one month; from-there I-went with-him to Troy, N.-Y., and-stayed there two-months; from'-there I-went with-him to Cohoes, N.-Y., and-stayed there two weeks; from-there I-went with-him 'to Providence, R. I., and'-stayed there about six weeks; from-there I-went with-him to Albany, N.-Y., and-stayed there about nine weeks.

Q. What-was-the' character (of the) business and-the nature of-your-employment at each-of these-places? A. We-were selling tea-and coffee at $1.00 a' can and-purchasers found presents in-every can. I-was employed as salesman at each-of these-places.

Q. How did-you-come to-go'-to Albany? A. I-went-there by-order of Mr. Mason.

Q. Who were-your fellow employees at-the Albany store? A. W. H. Henry', Stewart Williams, Edward Lawrence, Matthew Frazier, and F. D. Porter.

Q. What-was-the position of-each-one relative to-the business there? A. They'-were all salesmen like myself, with-the exception of F. D. Porter, who-was cashier.

Q. State-whether-you ever heard Mason assert or declare' anything about-the ownership (of the) Albany store?

Mr. Scott — I object to-that question.

The Court — The objection is overruled.

Mr. Scott — I-take'-an exception.

The Witness — He-told-me in Philadelphia for-(the)-first-time,[34] that-he-was-the proprietor (of the) Importers' Tea Company, then doing' business in Albany.

Q. Was-there any-one present at-this-time except Mason and-yourself? A. No,·sir. He-told-me this when-we'-were alone.

---

34. *For-the-first-time.* See p. 101, line 10.

Q. Do-you-know J. W. Smith? A. I-do.

Q. What relationship does he-bear to-the plaintiff in-this-action? A'. He-is-the son of Edward W. Smith.

Q. Were-you present when-the seizure was-made by-the sheriff of Albany County? A. I'-was.

Q. State who were present at-the-time of-such seizure. A. W. H. Henry, Stewart Williams, Edward Lawrence, Matthew Frazier, and F. D.' Porter.

Q. What-took-place and what-was-said relative thereto? A. I saw Richard F. Mason take-some-money out-of his pocket and'-hand it to Edward Smith, who placed it in-the cash-box and-afterwards took-it out and paid it to-the sheriff. This-was' after-the sheriff had notified R. F. Mason and Edward Smith that-he had levied on-their goods. After-the sheriff went out, Mason said'-that-that would-be-the last attachment and-said "that's-the-way I-do business, boys," addressing this to-the clerks.

Q. Were-you-present' when-the sheriff was paid-the money, for-the taking of-which this-action is brought? A. I-was.

Q. Prior to-the payment of'-said-money to-the sheriff, did-you-know anything about-the levy about to-be-made? A. I-did.

Q. From whom did-you learn' about-it? A. Richard F. Mason told me that-he-expected an-attachment to-be-laid on-the goods that morning. but-there-would-be' no trouble, as he-would soon settle it and-they would-go right ahead.

Q. As-near-as you-can remember, what-day' did-you en-ter-the store at Albany? A. I-went to-the store at Albany about-the 1st of October, 1891.

Q. What-day' did you-leave? A. About-the last of No-vember, 1891.

Q. What-was-the-name or style under-which-the busi-ness was carried on' at Albany? A. The Importers' Tea Company. (1,057.)

Eulogy on Washington.

Speech in-honor of-his Centennial Birth-day, delivered by Daniel Webster, at-a Public Dinner
in-the city of Washington, February 22', 1832.

I-rise, gentlemen, to-propose to-you the name of-that
great-man, in commemoration of whose birth, and-in-honor
of whose' character-and services, we-have here assembled.

I-am-sure that I express a-sentiment common to-every-
one present, when I-say-that there'-is-something-more-
than ordinarily solemn and-affecting in-this-occasion.

We-are met to testify our-regard for-him whose name is
intimately blended' with-whatever belongs most essentially
to-the prosperity, the liberty, the free institutions, and-the
renown of-our country. That name was of power to' rally
a-nation in-the hour of thick-thronging public disasters
and calamities; that name shone, amid-the storm of-war,
a-beacon light, to' cheer-and guide-the country's friends;
it flamed, too, like-a meteor, to-repel her foes. That name,
in-the days of peace, was-a' load-stone, attracting to itself
a whole people's confidence, a whole people's love, and-the
whole world's respect. That name, descending with-all-
time[35], spreading over'-the whole earth, and-uttered in-all-
the languages belonging to-the tribes and races of-men,
will forever be pronounced with affectionate gratitude by'-
every-one in whose breast there-shall arise an aspiration
for human rights and human liberty.

We perform this grateful duty, gentlemen, at-the expira-
tion' of-a hundred years from his birth, near-the place, so

---

35. *With-all-time,* THP-T-M.

cherished[36] and beloved by him, where his dust now re-
poses, and-in-the capital' which bears his-own immortal
name.

All experience evinces that human sentiments are
strongly influenced by associations. The recurrence of
anniversaries, or-of longer periods' of-time, naturally
freshens the recollection, and-deepens the impression, of
events with-which-they-are historically connected. Re-
nowned places, also, have-a power to' awaken feeling,
which all acknowledge. No American can pass by-the
fields of Bunker Hill, Monmouth, or Camden, as if-they-
were ordinary spots on'-the earth's surface. Whoever
visits them, feels the sentiment of-love of country kindling[37] anew, as if-the spirit that belonged to-the transac-
tions which'-have rendered these-places distinguished,
still hovered round, with power to-move-and excite all who
in future time may approach them.

But neither of'-these sources of emotion equals the
power with-which great moral examples affect-the mind.
When sublime virtues cease to-be abstractions, when-they
become' embodied[38] in human character, and exemplified
in human conduct, we should-be false to-our-own nature,
if-we-did not indulge in-the spontaneous'[39] effusions of-our
gratitude and our admiration. A-true lover (of the) virtue
of patriotism delights to contemplate its purest[40] models;
and-that love of' country may-be well suspected which af-
fects to soar so high into-the regions of sentiment as-to-be
lost and absorbed in-the abstract' feeling, and becomes too
elevated or too refined to-glow with fervor in-the commen-
dation (of the) love of individual benefactors[41]. All-this
is unnatural.' (525.)   *   *   *   *

---

36. *Cherished*, CH²-*R*-SHt.   40. *Purest*, P³-*R*st.   Written
37. *Kindling*, K¹-Nd-L-NG.   with upward *r* to distin-
38. *Embodied*, Mb¹-Dd.   guish it from *poorest*.
39. *Spontaneous*, sPnt¹-Ns.   41. *Benefactors*, Bn²-F-Ktrs.

SELF-RELIANCE.

BY R. W. EMERSON.

I read the-other-day[43] some verses written by-an eminent
painter which were original and-not conventional. Always
the soul hears an-admonition in'-such lines, let the subject
be what-it-may. The sentiment they instill is-of more-
value than any-thought they-may contain.   To-believe'
your-own thought, to-believe that what-is true for-you in-
your private heart is true for-all-men — that-is genius.
Speak your' latent conviction, and-it shall-be-the universal
sense; for always the inmost becomes the outmost — and
our first thought is rendered back to-us' by-the trumpets
(of the) Last Judgment. Familiar as-the voice (of the)
mind is to each, the highest merit we ascribe to Moses,
Plato', and Milton is-that-they set at naught books and-
traditions, and spoke not what men, but what they-thought.
A-man should learn to' detect and watch that gleam of
light which flashes across his mind from within, more-than
the lustre (of the) firmament of bards and sages'.   Yet he
dismisses without notice his thought, because it-is-his. In-
every work of genius we recognize our-own rejected
thoughts; they come back' to-us with-a certain alienated[44]
majesty. Great-works of art have-no-more affecting lesson for-us than this.   They teach us to abide' by-our spontaneous impression with good-humored inflexibility then
most when-the whole cry of voices is on-the-other-side.
Else to-morrow a stranger will'-say with masterly good-
sense precisely what we-have thought and-felt all-the time,
and-we-shall-be forced to-take with shame our'-own opinion
from another.

There-is-a time in-every-man's education when-he arrives

---

43. *The-other-day*, TIIthr-D.   44. *Alienated*, L²-N-Td.

at-the conviction that envy is ignorance; that imitation is'
suicide; that-he-must take himself for better for worse as-his
portion; that-though-the wide universe is full of good, no
kernel of' nourishing corn can come to-him but-through
his toil bestowed on-that plot of ground which-is given to-
him to till. The power' which resides in him is new in
nature, and-none but he knows what-that-is which he-can-
do, nor does he know until' he-has tried. Not for-nothing
one face, one character, one fact, makes much impression
on him, and another none. It-is-not without pre-established'[45] harmony, this sculpture[46] in-the memory. The
eye was placed where one ray should fall, that-it might testify of-that particular ray. Bravely let' him speak-the utmost syllable of-his confession. We but half express ourselves, and are ashamed of-that divine idea which each of-
us represents.' It-may-be safely trusted as proportionate
and-of good issues, so it-be faithfully imparted, but God
will-not-have his work made manifest' by cowards. It
needs-a divine man to exhibit anything divine. A-man is
relieved and gay when-he has put his heart into his' work
and-done his best; but what he-has said or done otherwise
shall give him no peace. It-is-a deliverance[47] which does-
not' deliver. In-the attempt his genius deserts him; no
muse befriends; no invention, no hope.

Trust thyself: every heart vibrates to-that iron string.
Accept'-the place the divine providence has-found for-you,
the society of-your contemporaries, the connection of
events. Great-men have-always done-so, and' confided
themselves childlike to-the genius of their-age, betraying
their perception that-the Eternal was stirring at-their heart,
working through-their hands, predominating'[48] in-all-their
being. (603.)   *   *   *   *

---

45. *Pre-established*, Pr¹ dis-   47. *Deliverance*, Dlns².
    joined St².   48. *Predominating*, Prd¹-Mn
46. *Sculpture*, sKl-Ptr².   T-ND.

· BUSINESS LETTERS ·

No.1 - Advertising

No.2 - Banking

No.3 - Book Publishing

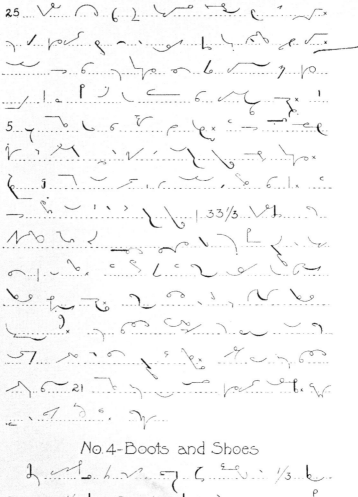

No. 4-Boots and Shoes

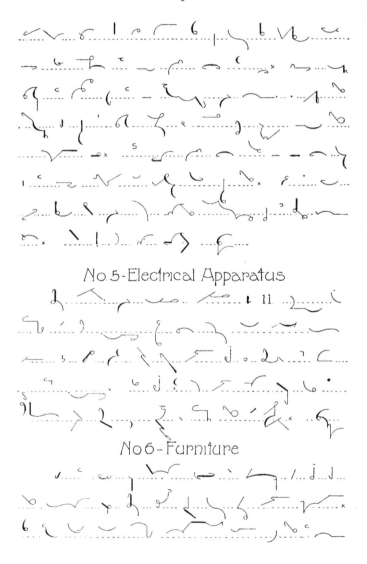

No. 5 - Electrical Apparatus

No. 6 - Furniture

No.7- Grain

No 8 - Hardware

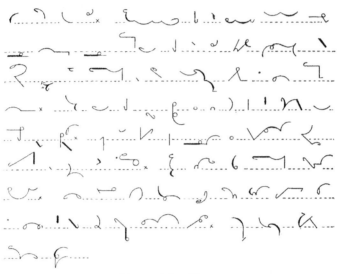

No 9 - Heating

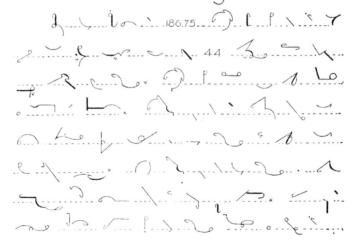

186.75

44

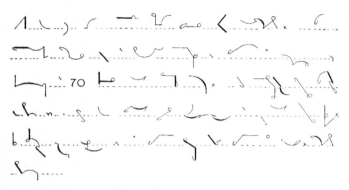

No 10 - Insurance

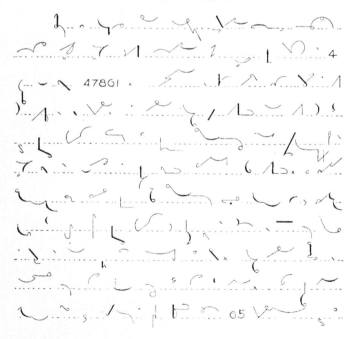

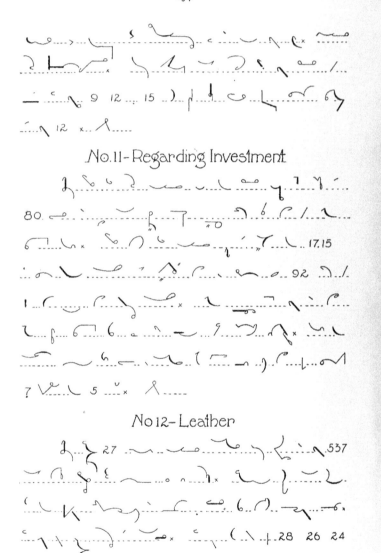

No.11- Regarding Investment

No 12- Leather

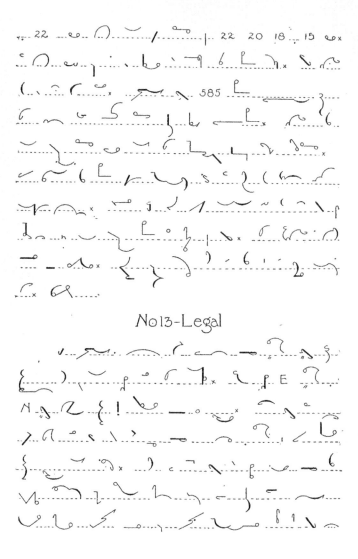

No 13-Legal

No.14–Legislative

157

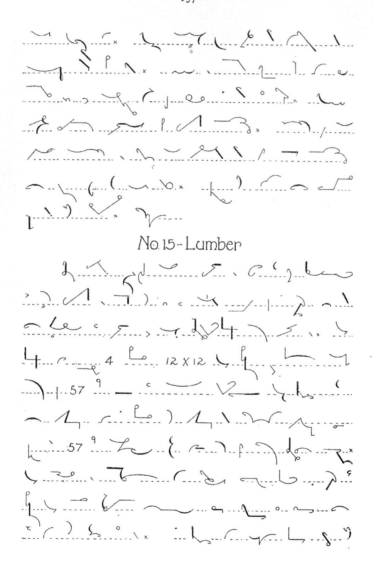

No. 15 - Lumber

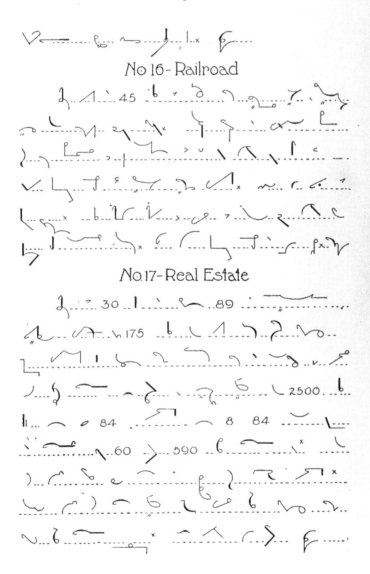

No 16 - Railroad

No. 17 - Real Estate

Testimony

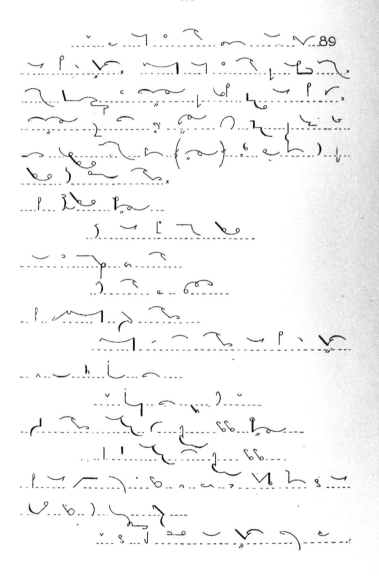

89

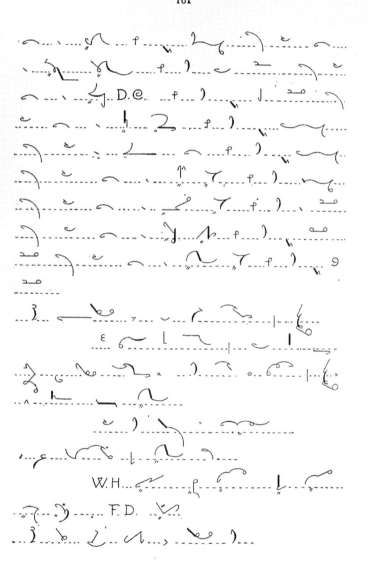

F. D.

J. W.

W. H.

F. D.

R.F.

1

91

91

Eulogy on Washington

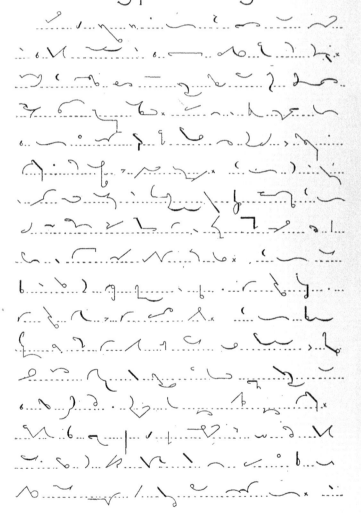

Self Reliance

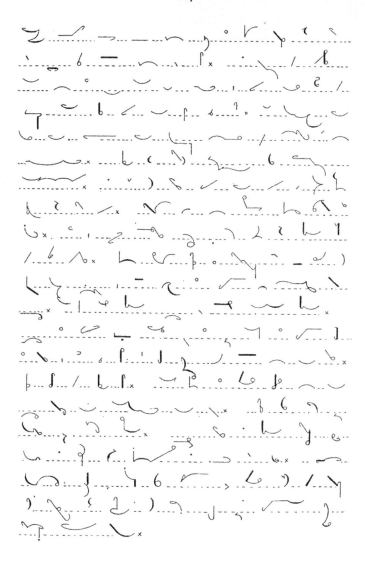

Abbreviations

advance	confidential-ly	domestic
advanced	congregate-d	eccentric-ity
advances	conspicuous-ly	electric al / ity
advantageous-ly	dangerous	emphatic al / ly
aggregate-d	decapitate-d	enthusiasm-tic
antagonize d / ism	delight-ed	entire
approximate d / ly	delinquent ly / cy	especial-ly
architect ure / nral	democrat-ic	essential-ly
aristocrat-ic	designate d / tion	executor
auspicious-ly	determine	executrix
bank	determination	extemporaneous ly
bankrupt	dignity fy / fied	extinct
bankruptcy	dilapidate d / tion	extraordinary ily
baptize d / ist	diplomat-ic	fastidious-ly
benevolent ly / ence	disadvantage	hospitable y / ity
benignant-ity	discrepant-cy	independent ly / ce
collect-ed	discriminate-d ly / tion	indifferent

Abbreviations

indignant-ly	magnetic	reform-ed
indiscriminate ly	magnetism	reformation
infinite-ly	manufacture-d	republic
infinitesimal-ly	manuscript	republican
influential	messenger	repugnant ly ce
inheritance	mortgage-d	require
inquire	neglect-ed	requirement
inst.	next	respect-ed ful ly
instinct ive ively	passenger	respective-ly
intellect ual ually	perpendicular-ly	satisfy actory ily
intimidate d tion	perpetual ly ate	special-ly
irrespective-ly	perspicuous ly ity	stenographer
irresponsible	plenipotentiary	substantial
jurisdiction	practicable y ility	territory
jurisprudence	preliminary	tranquil ly ity
magazine	privilege-d	transfer
magnanimous ly ity	prospect ed ive	unreasonable

Phrases

	your favor		First National Bank
	your valued favor		Savings Bank
	esteemed favor		General Superintendent
	we regret		& Co.
	we received		in our
	Yours truly		in our store
	Yours respectfully		at our store
	Very respectfully yours		at my store
	there are some		wholesale store
	there are as many as		such will
	there are several		which will have
	We are, Respectfully yours		it will have
	if it is not		try to have
	we think there is no		we hope you will conclude
	in which they are not		as early as possible
	yes sir		for some time
	no sir		give this matter

Printed in Great Britain
by Amazon

42531839R00099